ISSUES THAT CONCERN YOU

Birth Control

Roman Espejo, *Book Editor*

GREENHAVEN PRESS
A part of Gale, Cengage Learning

GALE
CENGAGE Learning·

Detroit • New York • San Francisco • New Haven, Conn • Waterville, Maine • London

Elizabeth Des Chenes, *Director, Publishing Solutions*

For more information, contact:
Greenhaven Press
27500 Drake Rd.
Farmington Hills, MI 48331-3535
Or you can visit our Internet site at gale.cengage.com

For product information and technology assistance, contact us at

Gale Customer Support, 1-800-877-4253
For permission to use material from this text or product, submit all requests online at www.cengage.com/permissions

Further permissions questions can be e-mailed to permissionrequest@cengage.com

Articles in Greenhaven Press anthologies are often edited for length to meet page requirements. In addition, original titles of these works are changed to clearly present the main thesis and to explicitly indicate the author's opinion. Every effort is made to ensure that Greenhaven Press accurately reflects the original intent of the authors. Every effort has been made to trace the owners of copyrighted material.

Cover image © Liv friis-larsen/Shutterstock.com.

LIBRARY OF CONGRESS CATALOGING-IN-PUBLICATION DATA

Birth control / Roman Espejo, book editor.
   p. cm. -- (Issues that concern you)
 Includes bibliographical references and index.
 ISBN 978-0-7377-5689-0 (hardcover)
 1. Birth control. 2. Teenagers--Sexual behavior. 3. Sex instruction. I.
Espejo, Roman, 1977-
  HQ766.B479 2012
  304.6'66--dc23
                                   2011051625

Printed in the United States of America
1 2 3 4 5 6 7 16 15 14 13 12

CONTENTS

Although conservative and liberal stances differ on birth control and family planning, the prevailing opinion is that teenagers should practice abstinence, as they lack the maturity to make decisions that can have a lifelong impact or to handle the emotional intimacy and involvement of sexual intercourse. In fact, some researchers claim that the frontal lobe of the brain—which dictates judgment, problem solving, impulse control, and sexual behavior—is not fully developed until the mid-twenties.

Age is often just a number, however, and it does not instantly prepare an individual for sex and its responsibilities. Adults also deal with the consequences of failing to use birth control and other unwise sexual choices; for example, a study suggests that teens do not necessarily have more abortions than older women. Between 2000 and 2008 women aged twenty to twenty-four had the highest abortion rate, at 39.9 per 1,000, followed by women aged twenty-five to twenty-nine, at 28.6 per 1,000. The rate for women aged fifteen to nineteen came in third, at 19.8 per 1,000.

Still, with the negative impacts of an unplanned pregnancy on teens and their futures—higher dropout rates, diminished educational and professional opportunities, increased likelihood of poverty—their being given knowledge of and access to contraceptives is backed by numerous youth advocates and experts alike. The condom is the most accessible contraceptive method of all, sold at virtually all drug, convenience, and grocery stores without age restrictions. Many high schools, clinics, and youth centers routinely offer them for free, too. And unlike the pill, intrauterine devices (IUDs), and birth control shots, condoms are available without a prescription and offer some protection against sexually transmitted infections (STIs).

To teach young people about condoms, Karen Rayne, an expert on sex education and an adjunct professor at the University of Texas at Austin, took ten middle school students (with parental

The most readily available form of birth control is condoms, which are sold over the counter in drugstores and grocery stores, without age restrictions.

consent) to a pharmacy to buy condoms. According to Rayne in her blog post about the field trip, the students were concerned that the clerks would refuse to sell them condoms or ask them what they were for. None of them, however, ran into any problems. "Neither of the clerks who checked them out made any comment," Rayne notes. "One student said, 'It was no different than if I had just been buying a Coke!'" she adds. When they returned to the classroom, Rayne demonstrated the proper use of the latex barriers. "Buying condoms and learning how to use them correctly has not made these students any more likely to actually use condoms. But now they all know exactly how to use condoms correctly when the time does come," she maintains.

Rayne's lesson in buying and using condoms drew opposition as well as approval on her blog. "If the parents are so excited about their children learning how to purchase and use condoms, they should be the ones to go with their child," wrote one commentator. On the other hand, the mother of a boy who went on the field trip believed it educated her son. "When our child actually does have sex for the first time years from now," she stated, "he can remember back to this class and think, 'Oh, I have bought condoms before. It was not a big deal. I can easily do it again.'"[1]

These two statements reflect opposing views on teaching students about condoms. The first response supports the position of opponents that minors' accessibility to birth control is a parental right and responsibility, not the place of a school or clinic. Another argument is that the contraceptive is ineffective in preventing pregnancy; some statistics report that condoms may fail at a relatively high rate when not used correctly and consistently. In such "typical" use, the failure rate is 17.4 per 100, comparable to 18.4 per 100 for withdrawal before ejaculation. Finally, some contend that the increased accessibility to condoms leads to promiscuity. A British study concluded that sexual activity and STIs (sexually transmitted infections) among adolescents rose in areas that offered expanded free birth control programs.

The second response supports the position of advocates that teens should be taught where to get condoms and how to use them properly, as condoms are often the first line of defense against unplanned pregnancy and for practicing safer sex for sexually active youths, given their low cost and easy access. Regarding the effectiveness of condoms, one estimate claims that in one year, 15 percent of women who do not use any birth control will not become pregnant, which is lower than the success rate of typical condom use (17.4 percent). Likewise, the link between condom availability and promiscuity is also disputed. A study published in 2007 determined that teens who used condoms the first time they had sex had lower rates of STIs and the same number of partners compared with those who did not use them.

Birth control for teens is not a black-and-white issue. While the topic might cause embarrassment for some, it is vital for students to get accurate information and a balanced view of the arguments and evidence. This volume presents a variety of viewpoints about the methods of contraception as well as on sex education, abstinence, and birth control programs and policies. Also, it offers a bibliography of books and articles for more research as well as a list of organizations to contact for additional information. Lastly, the two-part appendix, What You Should Know About Birth Control and What You Should Do About Birth Control, gives young people statistics and facts and information on dealing with contraception. These features in *Issues That Concern You: Birth Control* provide a well-rounded view on this area of sexual health.

Note
1. Karen Rayne, "Buying Condoms? In Middle School?," *Adolescent Sexuality by Dr. Karen Rayne* (blog), April 1, 2009. http://karenrayne.com/2009/04/01/buying-condoms-in-middle-school.

ONE

Many Young Adults Are Unknowledgeable About Birth Control

Amanda Hess

Writer Amanda Hess covers sex and gender for TBD.com in Washington, DC In the following article Hess points out that young people—especially men—are uninformed about contraceptives and their functions. In dating and relationships, women frequently face confusion about the birth control pill and vaginal ring from their partners, she says. A survey also shows that men in their late teens and twenties have misperceptions about condoms and conception. The lack of awareness surrounding birth control sparks the examination of other issues, explains Hess, such as weighing the responsibilities of pregnancy protection and attitudes toward women's sexual health.

Allison, 26, and her boyfriend were having sex—an activity they had engaged in many times over the six months they had been dating—when her contraceptive vaginal ring fell right out of her vagina. Her boyfriend paused. He developed a sudden concern over the efficacy of the couple's method of birth control [BC]. "He was like, 'Oh, no. How is it going to catch my semen?'" Allison recalls.

For about a year now, Allison has used the NuvaRing to prevent pregnancy. Three weeks out of the month, the clear, flexible plastic ring sits in Allison's vagina and releases hormones into her bloodstream that prevent her from ovulating. It does not "catch" anybody's semen.

"He played it off as a joke," says Allison of her boyfriend's bizarre interpretation of her birth control. "But in the tone of his voice, that honest worry was there. Part of him was thinking, 'What does this ring actually do?'"

Allison is a veteran witness to contraception awareness syndrome, "I was dating a guy in college who knew that I was on the birth control pill. Of course, he was concerned about me getting pregnant," says Allison. "So he said, 'You know, you should take four or five of these a day—just take as many as you need to,'" she says.

Jenna had been living with her boyfriend for several months when he floated his own contraceptive theory. Jenna was taking her birth control pills continuously, meaning that she was skipping the pack's built-in placebo pills in order to stop her period. At some point, her boyfriend discovered how she had managed to avoid the monthly ritual. "I was thinking you were just magical, like a unicorn," he told her. "I mean, you hope one exists somewhere, but you never think you'll get to live with one . . . a cool chick with no period drama that has sex all month long." He added, "The guys thought I was making it up." (Boyfriends could not be reached for comment for this story.)

"Magical" Attitudes Toward Contraception

According to a new study by the National Campaign to Prevent Teen and Unplanned Pregnancy, many young American men exhibit attitudes toward contraception that could best be described as "magical." The study surveyed American singles ages 18–29 about their perceptions about and use of contraception. Twenty-eight percent of young men think that wearing two condoms at a time is more effective than just one. Twenty-five percent think that women can prevent pregnancy by douching after sex. Eighteen percent believe that they can reduce the chance of pregnancy by doing it standing up.

A survey has shown that men in their late teens and twenties have misconceptions about condoms and contraceptives.

For the most part, men lagged behind women on the pregnancy prevention front. And when the study dipped into the realm of "female" forms of birth control, the gender divide intensified. In the study, 29 percent of men and 32 percent of women reported that they know "little or nothing about condoms." When asked to rate their knowledge of birth control pills, 78 percent of men reported to be clueless, compared to 45 percent of women.

With a majority of young men generally unknowledgeable about hormonal birth control—and nearly half of young women equally stumped—men sometimes don't figure out the basics until they think they may have impregnated someone, or their penis feels something weird. "I dated a girl with a NuvaRing, while I didn't know she had one," says a 22-year-old Arlington resident who didn't discover how the couple was preventing baby-making until his penis was already well inside her vagina. "I found out the physical way, when I felt the alien object. I immediately recoiled in fear, asking what was wrong. It was frightening. Then she told me her birth control was a ring in her vagina, which I had never heard of." He demanded the evidence. "She retrieved it—which is a sight to see—and showed it to me, put it back, and we continued," he says. "I feel like girls should tell people."

When Allison's boyfriend expressed concern with the efficacy of her vaginal ring, she told him all about it. But even between two adults, the subject inspired some awkwardness. "The conversation wasn't exactly freeflowing," Allison says. "I've been dating since high school, and it feels like the men that I date now have a very similar idea of birth control as the men I dated who were high school students," says Allison. "They get a preliminary idea in sex ed, and then there's not really any education after that. Nothing ever changes."

Responsibilities for Pregnancy Prevention

In addition to staging teach-ins, women are also responsible for shouldering the physical, emotional, and financial responsibilities for pregnancy prevention. Pap smears, STI [sexually transmitted infection] tests, and gynecological sessions about their contraceptive options—that's just the tip of it for the sexually active woman. In order to keep their birth control subscription fresh, they have to repeat that process every year. Their male sex partners are under no such requirements. As *Salon* noted last year [2009] women have 11 methods of contraception from which to choose; men have two—condom and vasectomy. And even if men did have additional reliable birth control options, many women wouldn't trust them to use them correctly. In a comment on the *Salon* article, one woman wrote, "I love my husband more than anything in the world but I would not place that responsibility on him because if the BC failed and he was

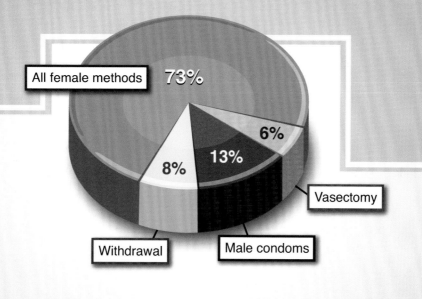

Method of Birth Control Used in Developed Countries

These data come from the United Nations Population Division's *World Contraceptive Use*, 2003.

All female methods 73%

6%

13%

8%

Vasectomy

Withdrawal

Male condoms

Taken from: International Male Contraception Coalition. "Will Women Trust Men to Use New Male Contraceptives?" 2003. www.imccoalition.org/facts/Attitudes_toward_male_contraception.pdf.

responsible for it I would kill him then he would be dead and I would be having a child while in prison." Perhaps it is no mystery why some men confine their responsibility to forms of birth control which relate directly to their own genitalia.

Gustav Seestedt, 23, says that birth control pills are the form of contraception he has "the most indirect experience with." He has no idea how they work. "I thought it, uh, controlled, uh . . . I actually don't know, now that I think about it," he says. "Oh, man, I thought it had something to do with hormonal control, but that doesn't seem right at all. That sounds pretty awful. I thought it, uh, somehow killed fertility with like chemicals and stuff," he says. The ring, however, strikes Seestedt as a superior option. "I thought that was pretty fine, because, from what I understood, it was kind of a low-cost way of doing it, and it wasn't really . . . I like it because chemical pills and stuff are kind of weird, [but the ring] was kind of placed inside, and . . . you know what I mean? It just kind of did its thing, you know?"

A Juvenile Disregard

To some, the male indifference to birth control can be attributed to a juvenile disregard for all things related to the place in which the vaginal ring "does its thing." We live in a country where heterosexual heartthrob Robert Pattinson feels comfortable announcing to *Details* magazine, "I really hate vaginas. I'm allergic to vagina." Where tech nerds everywhere let out a collective titter over new Apple device the "iPad," because it sounds kind of like a thing women use when they're on their periods. Where [director] Judd Apatow has built a film career out of turning extended vagina jokes into blockbusters.

"I definitely think that the inability to understand birth control goes back to the woman's period," says Allison. Months after the vaginal ring incident, Allison's boyfriend remained confused about the specifics of her menstrual cycle. "The other day, I was on my period, and I took out my tampon before I went into the shower," she says. "My boyfriend was like, 'Wait: But you just took your tampon out. Can you go into the shower like that?'"

Allison responded to her boyfriend's question with more questions. "Does he think that the second I take out my tampon, it's just blood, blood everywhere?" she wondered. "That if I don't plug it up with this cotton thing every moment, all hell will break loose?" Her boyfriend did not elaborate. "He was just kind of like, 'Never mind,'" says Allison. "I think he understood the absurdity of his comment. But he was making an honest attempt to learn about something he doesn't really know about."

TWO

Abstinence-Only Education Does Not Teach the Effective Use of Birth Control

Advocates for Youth

> While most Americans agree that teens should be abstinent until marriage, in reality the majority has sex out of wedlock. Advocates for Youth, a nonprofit organization that promotes access to and education on birth control, contends that teaching only abstinence before marriage withholds vital information about birth control as well as about pregnancy, abortion, sexually transmitted infections (STIs), and sexual orientation from young people. Participants in abstinence-only programs may delay sexual activity longer, claims Advocates for Youth, but they have similar rates of unplanned pregnancies and STIs due to their lack of knowledge and usage of birth control. The following viewpoint by Advocates for Youth presents evidence for this position and other arguments regarding the ineffectiveness of abstinence-only programs in helping teens make informed choices about sex.

The vast majority of Americans support abstinence from sexual activity for school-age children, especially younger adolescents. Yet, abstinence-only-until-marriage programs, currently being taught in many schools, are at odds with what most Americans want schools to teach. The public supports a broad sex education curriculum that stresses abstinence as the best way to avoid unintended pregnancy and sexually transmitted infections (STIs) but that also conveys complete and medically accurate information about contraception and condoms.

Despite these strong public preferences, the federal government has invested more than $1.5 billion in state and federal dollars since 1997 into prescriptive abstinence-only and abstinence-only-until-marriage programs that are, at best, ineffective and wasteful and, at worst, misleading and dangerous to America's youth.

Critics argue that abstinence-only programs withhold vital information about issues such as birth control, sexually transmitted infections, abortion, and sexual orientation.

Federally funded abstinence-only programs must adhere to a stringent eight-point definition of education. Funded programs must have the "exclusive purpose of teaching the social, psychological, and health gains to be realized by abstaining from sexual activity." They must teach, among other things, that "sexual activity outside of marriage may have harmful psychological and physical effects" and that "a mutually faithful monogamous relationship in the context of marriage is the expected standard for all school-age children." This eight-point definition isn't based on evidence-based, public health and social science research. Rather, it reflects and promotes a socially conservative "values" agenda put forward by ultraconservative members of Congress. Program guidelines explicitly prohibit any discussion of contraceptives, except for failure rates. This limitation is particularly problematic for sexually experienced adolescents, a group with reproductive health needs distinctly different from the needs of sexually inexperienced youth. By emphasizing marriage as the expected standard, programs also exclude gay, lesbian, bisexual, transgender and questioning [LGBTQ] youth and ignore their needs.

False, Misleading, or Distorted Information

A few of the reasons—practical, public health, and ethical—for questioning public investments in abstinence-only-until-marriage programs are outlined below.

Many abstinence-only curricula contain "false, misleading or distorted information." A 2004 investigation by the minority staff of the House Government Reform Committee reviewed 13 commonly used abstinence-only curricula taught to millions of school-age youth. The study concluded that two of the curricula were accurate but that 11 others, used by 69 organizations in 25 states, blurred religion and science, and contained unproven claims and subjective conclusions or outright falsehoods regarding the effectiveness of contraceptives, gender traits, and when life begins. Among the misconceptions and outright falsehoods:

- A 43-day-old fetus is a "thinking person."
- HIV [the AIDS virus] can be spread via sweat and tears.

- Half of gay male teenagers in the United States have tested positive for HIV.
- Pregnancy can result from touching another person's genitals.
- Condoms fail to prevent HIV transmission as often as 31 percent of the time in heterosexual intercourse.
- Women who have an abortion "are more prone to suicide."
- As many as 10 percent of women who have an abortion become sterile.

Government has an obligation to provide accurate information and to eschew the provision of misinformation. Such obligations extend to state-supported health education and health care services. By providing misinformation and withholding accurate information that youth need to make informed choices, abstinence-only-until-marriage programs violate youth's basic human right to sexual health information, are ethically unsupportable, and inherently coercive. Health care providers and health educators have ethical obligations to provide accurate health information. Patients and students have a right to receive the most accurate and complete information—information that will allow young people to achieve good health outcomes. Current federal abstinence laws and guidelines are ethically problematic because they limit the information—including accurate information about contraception and safer sex—available to young people.

No Impact on Desired Outcomes

There is no evidence to date that abstinence-only-until-marriage programs bring about the desired long-term behavioral outcomes at which they aim—outcomes such as delays in sexual activity and reductions in unintended pregnancies and STIs. Although abstinence-only-until-marriage programs have the enthusiastic backing of some right-wing constituencies, the congressionally mandated, long-term evaluation of four highly touted abstinence-only programs (finally released in April 2007) does *not* support continued funding. The study found that programs had no impact on desired behavioral outcomes. Programs did not achieve later sexual initiation or lower rates of pregnancy or STIs. By the end of the study, abstinence-only participants had their first sexual encounter at the same average age as the control group. In both the control group and study group, only 23 percent reported always using a condom when having sex. Other recent research shows that abstinence-only strategies may deter contraceptive use among sexually active teens, increasing their risk of unintended pregnancy and STIs.

Considerable scientific evidence demonstrates that programs that include information about both abstinence and contraception can work to help teens delay sexual activity, have fewer sexual partners and increase contraceptive use when they begin having sex. Although there is no one silver bullet, effective programs include curriculum-based sex education that includes information about *both* abstinence and contraceptive use. Other effective approaches include youth development programs whose primary focus is to engage young people constructively in their communities and schools. Another approach, shown to be effective with girls, combines health care, academic assistance, comprehensive sex education, participation in performing arts and individual sports, and employment assistance. Researchers have also identified certain characteristics of effective curricula. These programs:

- Have a narrow focus and a clear message that not having sex or that using contraception consistently and carefully is the right thing to do;
- Last more than a few weeks;
- Address peer pressure;
- Teach communication skills;
- Reflect the age, sexual experience, and culture of young people in the program.

The public prefers comprehensive sex education to abstinence-only-until-marriage programs by a wide margin. According to a poll, conducted in 2003 by the Kaiser Family Foundation, National Public Radio, and Harvard University, only 15 percent of Americans believe that schools should only teach abstinence from sexual intercourse and should not provide information on condoms and other contraception. A 2007 poll of voters conducted by the National Women's Law Center and Planned Parenthood Federation of America yielded remarkably similar results, with more than three out of four respondents preferring comprehensive sex education curricula, while only 14 percent favored an "abstinence-only" approach.

Americans expressed support for a broad sex education curriculum that teaches about abstinence as well as the "basics of how babies are made." In addition,

- 99 percent of Americans wanted programs to cover other STIs as well as HIV.
- 98 percent wanted youth to learn all about HIV and AIDS.
- 94 percent wanted youth to learn how to get tested for HIV and other STIs.
- 93 percent wanted youth to be taught about "waiting to have sexual intercourse until married."
- 83 percent wanted youth to learn how to put on a condom.
- 71 percent wanted youth to know that "teens can obtain birth control pills from family planning clinics without permission from a parent."

The Kaiser poll also found that that a substantial plurality (46 percent) believes that the most appropriate approach is "abstinence-plus." These Americans felt that schools should emphasize abstinence but should also teach about condoms and contraception. Thirty-six percent of those polled believed that abstinence is *not* the most important thing, and that sex education should focus on teaching teens how to make responsible decisions about sex.

Despite clear evidence of failure, the U.S. government continues to fund and promote abstinence-only-until-marriage programs. This illogical promotion and funding crowds out effective approaches to health education and related services. Increasingly, abstinence-only-until-marriage education is replacing more comprehensive sex education in the nation's schools. In 1999, 23 percent of sex education teachers in secondary schools taught abstinence as the only way to prevent pregnancy and STIs, compared with only two percent who had done so in 1988. Between 1995 and

Who Designs Sex Education Programs?

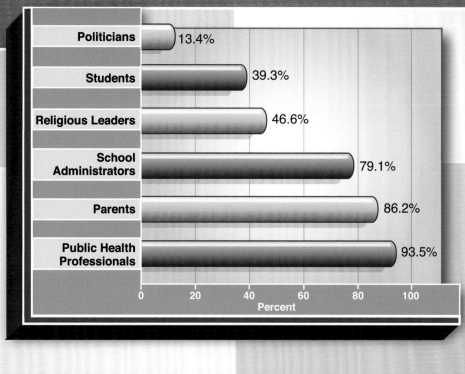

Parents who thought sexual education should be taught in schools believe the following groups should decide *how* it is taught:

Group	Percent
Politicians	13.4%
Students	39.3%
Religious Leaders	46.6%
School Administrators	79.1%
Parents	86.2%
Public Health Professionals	93.5%

Taken from: Adolescent Pregnancy Prevention Campaign of North Carolina. "What Do Parents Think About Sex Education?" Parent Survey 2009.

2002, the proportion of adolescents who had received any formal instruction about methods of birth control declined significantly (from 81 percent to 66 percent of males and from 87 percent to 70 percent for females). By 2002, one-third of adolescents of each gender had not received any instruction about birth control methods. . . .

Abstinence-only until-marriage programs violate free speech. Federally funded programs restrict young people's access to much-needed health information and limit their education to the "approved" messages in the government's definition of abstinence-only education. As a result, recipients of federal abstinence-only funds as well as the teachers who provide federally funded health education to their students operate under a gag order that censors the communication of vital sexual health information. . . .

Public Health Principles, Not Ideology

Abstinence-only-until-marriage as a method of birth control is spectacularly ineffective. Like other methods, abstinence-only-until-marriage works if "used" consistently and correctly. Common sense as well as available research, suggests that in the real world, it can and does fail routinely—as evidenced by the staggering proportion (95 percent) of Americans who have had premarital sex. A recent study of teens who made a public pledge to abstain until marriage questioned the youth again six years after they made the pledge. Researchers found that over 60 percent had broken their vow to remain abstinent until marriage. The study also found that teens who took virginity pledges begin engaging in vaginal intercourse later than non-pledging teens, but that pledgers were more likely to engage in oral or anal sex than non-pledging virgin teens and less likely to use condoms once they become sexually active. The study found that pledgers were much less likely than non-pledgers to use contraception the first time they had sex and also were less likely than other teens to have undergone STI testing and to know their STI status. As a result, the STI rates between pledgers and non-pledgers were statistically similar.

Virtually all Americans have sex before marrying—a fact that has been true since the 1950s. The unrealistic, morality-based agenda that abstinence-only programs are attempting to promote runs counter to the life choices of almost all Americans. The present median age of sexual initiation is 17 and the average age of marriage is 25.8 for women and 27.4 for men, meaning that the length of time between sexual onset and marriage is eight to 10 years on average. The gap between sexual onset and marriage has increased across time, and premarital sex is an almost universal practice. By age 20, 75 percent of Americans have had sex before marriage; the percentage rises to 95 percent of Americans by age 44. Even among those who abstained from sex until age 20 or older, 81 percent have had premarital sex by age 44.

Given that half of teens have had sex, even when educators encourage them not to, sex education must be driven by public health principles rather than ideology. Sex education may promote abstinence as the best option for teens. But given that so many students will not abstain from sex, programs have an obligation to help teens understand the risks and responsibilities that come with sex. Survey after survey indicates that adolescents have a tremendous unmet need for information related to sexuality, contraception, STIs, and making sexual decisions. Government-sponsored programs need to fill this information gap, not cause it to worsen.

A nationwide survey conducted by the Kaiser Family Foundation and *Seventeen* magazine revealed considerable gaps in teens' knowledge. The survey found that many teens hold misconceptions and harbor unnecessary and unfounded fears—such as the belief that contraception can cause infertility or birth defects. Nearly 20 percent of surveyed teens underestimated the effectiveness of the contraceptive patch or ring, and over 25 percent believed that emergency contraception causes abortion. Few teens understood the effectiveness of the male condom in preventing STIs, including HIV. In addition, over 25 percent of the teens did not know that oral contraception provides no protection against sexually transmitted diseases. The government-sponsored abstinence evaluation conducted by Mathematica Policy Research also confirmed that teens have important gaps in knowledge of STIs. The study found that on average, youth got only about half the answers correct regarding the health consequences of STIs.

More Information and Services Needed

Public health statistics confirm the need for more, not less, information and services directed at adolescents.

- About three out of 10 young women become pregnant at least once before they reach the age of 20—approximately 750,000 per year. Eight in 10 of these pregnancies are unintended.

- Approximately a quarter of teen females and 18 percent of teen males did not use a method of contraception at first intercourse.
- The interval between the time an adolescent female starts sexual activity and seeks health care services is approximately 12 months.
- About 20 percent of adolescent pregnancies occur within one month of the onset of sexual activity, and 50 percent occur within six months.
- Adolescents are at higher risk for acquiring STIs for a combination of behavioral, biological, and cultural reasons. The higher prevalence reflects: 1) multiple barriers to accessing quality STI prevention services, including lack of insurance or other ability to pay; 2) lack of transportation; 3) discomfort with facilities and services designed for adults; and 4) concerns about confidentiality.
- An estimated half of all new HIV infections occur in people under age 25.
- Recent estimates suggest that while representing 25 percent of the ever sexually active population, 15- to 24-year olds acquire nearly one-half of all new STIs.

Recent strides in reducing adolescent pregnancy are almost exclusively a function of contraceptive use. Improved contraceptive use is responsible for 86 percent of the decline in the U.S. adolescent pregnancy rate between 1995 and 2002. Only 14 percent of the change among 15- to 19-year-old women was attributable to a decrease in the percentage who were sexually active. Even though the birth rate for teenagers fell to 40.4 births per 1,000 women aged 15–19 in 2005, the lowest in 65 years, the United States continues to have the highest teenage birth rate of any of the world's developed nations.

Discriminatory by Definition

Abstinence-only-until-marriage programs are of little value to sexually active teens and, by definition, discriminate against lesbian, gay, bisexual, and transgender youth. Adolescents are often reluctant to acknowledge sexual activity, seek out contraception, and/or discuss sexuality, even in the most open settings. Abstinence-only programs do *not* provide a much-needed forum in which sexually active adolescents can address critical issues—such as safer sex, the benefits of contraception, legal rights to health care, and ways to access reproductive health services. Instead, abstinence-only programs allow discussions only within the narrow limits developed by conservatives in Congress.

For gay, lesbian and bisexual teens and for those struggling with their sexual orientation or sexual identity, the abstinence-only-until-marriage approach is even more harmful. Programs typically teach students that homosexuality is deviant and immoral. They promote marriage as a much-desired heterosexual institution. Consequently, programs ignore the emotional or health needs of LGBTQ youth, denigrating them even while giving them a daunting choice—pretend to be straight or remain celibate forever. . . .

Promoting marriage as the only acceptable family structure denigrates the choice of many Americans to be single or live in nontraditional arrangements.

Despite the message of abstinence-only-until-marriage programs that marriage is the expected standard of human behavior, individuals should have the right—without governmental interference or proselytizing—to determine if and/or when marriage may be an appropriate or desirable life choice. The number of Americans who are unmarried and single has been growing steadily in recent years, reaching 89.8 million in 2005, and including 41 percent of all U.S. residents age 18 and older. In 2005, 55 million households were headed by unmarried men or women—49 percent of households nationwide; and 12.9 million single parents lived with their children. Nearly 30 million people lived alone (26 percent of all households), up from 17 percent in 1970. Forty percent of opposite-sex, unmarried-partner households included children.

THREE

Parents Must Provide Guidance About Sex and Birth Control

Shari Rudavsky

In the following article Shari Rudavsky, who writes about health and medicine for the *Indiana Star*, emphasizes the importance of ongoing, early parental guidance of teens on birth control and sex. Whether discussing birth control options or abstinence until marriage, parents have more influence on their children's choices involving sex and intimacy than their peers do, says Rudavsky. Both daughters and sons must be addressed about pregnancy and methods of contraception. But some parents, Rudavsky suggests, do not believe they are the only adults who can guide teens through these issues.

Talking with one's children about sex is awkward enough. Talking with one's children about birth control can be that much more uncomfortable for parent, child or both. Yet, experts recommend that parents start having these conversations—in an age-appropriate fashion—long before a child is old enough to be sexually active. Such discussions will pave the way for a parent to ensure that his or her sexually active child takes precautions to protect against pregnancy and disease.

"Parents should disabuse themselves of this notion that it is a one-time talk. It is and should be an 18-year conversation," said

Bill Albert, chief program officer for the National Campaign to Prevent Teen and Unplanned Pregnancy. Despite parents' fears that their teens tune out everything they say, studies have shown how much such conversations matter. Parents influence children's decisions about sex more than their peers, Albert said. And despite parents' fears that talking about sex may encourage their teens to engage in it, studies show this is not the case.

A Two-Part Message

Teens can accept a two-part message that says on the one hand, "Please delay having sex, but if you do have sex, use contraception," Albert said. "Parents need to keep in mind that they don't actually have control over this unless they exert such extreme

Parents may feel uncomfortable discussing birth control with their children, but such conversations are necessary to ensure that teenagers take precautions against pregnancy and disease.

control over their child that they chaperone them," said Dr. J. Dennis Fortenberry, a professor of pediatrics at the Indiana University School of Medicine and adolescent medicine specialist. "What they need to do is give their young person enough tools to be safe."

And odds are, a teenager, especially an older one, is having sex, said Dr. Margaret Blythe, adolescent medicine specialist at Riley Hospital for Children in Indianapolis. Parents may concentrate efforts on their daughters, fearing they will become pregnant. But sons also need to learn about birth control, especially methods that keep them protected from sexually transmitted diseases. About 4 percent of youth have chlamydia at any time.

"We need to treat sex as something different than drugs, alcohol and other risk behaviors," said Blythe, a professor of pediatrics at the Indiana University School of Medicine. "It's part of our lives, and it should be a healthy part." But many parents believe sex should not be a part of their children's lives until marriage.

Parent-Teen Communication

About four in ten teens have intercourse before talking to parents about birth control, safe sex, and sexually transmitted infections. This statistic comes from a survey of the Talking Parents, Healthy Teens program.

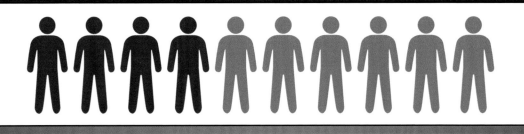

Taken from: Alice Park, "Parents' Sex Talk with Kids: Too Little, Too Late." *Time*, December 7, 2009.

The best way to ensure that is to talk with your teens from an early age about your values, encouraging them to adopt them, said Valerie Huber, executive director of the National Abstinence Education Association. However, talking about abstinence does not mean ignoring other sex-related topics. Parents may want to cite statistics that indicate about two-thirds of teens who have had sex wish they had waited. Or they can discuss contraception and how it may reduce but not eliminate the risk of pregnancy.

Once a teen has sex, he or she should see a doctor, but parents need not give up hope that the teen might return to abstinence or at least limit the number of future partners, Huber said. The important thing is to keep talking, lest the teen go elsewhere for advice. Not every parent takes the stance that he or she is the only adult in a child's life who can guide him or her through this topic.

Leah Jackman-Wheitner does not need to be the one her two daughters go to with questions about birth control. The mother of a 12- and 14-year-old, Jackman-Wheitner tries to convey the importance of being in a relationship with a person with whom one can communicate. She also encouraged her older daughter to participate in a church program that emphasized self-respect and making good choices.

FOUR

Clinics and Schools Can Help Improve Birth Control Services

Randi Burlew and Susan Philliber

> Randi Burlew is a senior research associate at Philliber Research Associates (PRA), a firm that evaluates human service, health, and education organizations. Susan Philliber is a partner at PRA. The following selection, which Burlew and Philliber wrote for the National Campaign to Prevent Teen and Unplanned Pregnancy, describes the characteristics and practices of effective birth control services for youths. Birth control services can be placed in three categories: clinic-based interventions, school-based and school-linked interventions, and interventions that use trained peer "providers." Success in pregnancy prevention, the authors state, is seen with a wide range of flexible and confidential services as well as education programs, the availability of contraceptives, and outreach to young people.

The most effective teen clinic programs can be placed into one of three categories:

1. Clinic-based interventions offer family planning and sexually transmitted infection (STI) prevention services to teenagers. Some of these programs have been developed for adult and teen clients while others are specifically designed for

teens. These interventions can take many forms. Some are developed to offer low (or no) cost, confidential, comprehensive family planning and reproductive health services to teenagers who might not otherwise have access to them. Other programs offer pregnancy and STI prevention interventions (e.g., videos, literature, classes) in addition to, or as a part of, standard health care visits. The actual services that are provided can vary widely based on the type of agency that operates the clinic (e.g., health departments, Planned Parenthood affiliates, and independent agencies). A 2003 survey of publicly funded clinics showed that more than 90% of clinics offer oral contraceptives, injectables, and condoms and 80% offer some type of emergency contraception. Further, three-quarters offer the contraceptive patch and four out of ten offer the vaginal ring. These agencies also provide other routine tests and procedures, the most common of which are pelvic exams, STI screening and treatment, breast examinations, and Pap smears. Another common feature of family planning clinics is that they may offer several important programs for teenagers including school outreach and education programs that focus on postponing sexual intercourse.

2. School-based and school-linked interventions consist of clinics that are either located within a school or within close proximity to a school. Research has consistently shown that school-based and school-linked clinics do not increase the proportion of teens who are sexually experienced. The most effective of these programs provide information about both abstinence and contraception and they focus on behavior. [Researcher D.] Kirby notes that school-based and school-linked clinics offer several advantages over traditional clinics, including: they provide easy access for youth, they serve both boys and girls, they offer a wide range of services, their services are confidential and often free, and their staff is skilled at working with youth. In addition, school-based and school-linked clinics have greater access to students for follow up and for providing educational programs. The primary disadvantage of school-based clinics is that they only serve those teens who are actually in school. In addition, though some reproductive health services

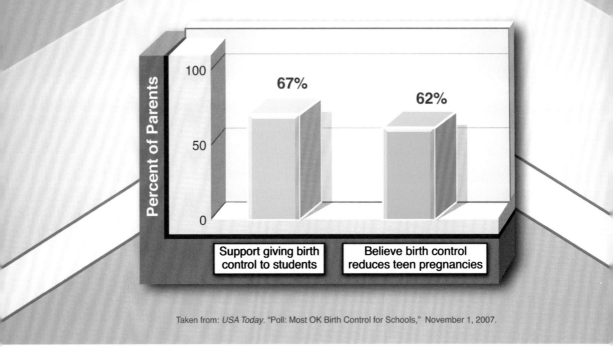

Parental Support of Birth Control in Schools

Data are based on an Associated Press–Ipsos poll.

Percent of Parents

- 100
- 67%
- 62%
- 50
- 0

Support giving birth control to students

Believe birth control reduces teen pregnancies

Taken from: *USA Today*. "Poll: Most OK Birth Control for Schools," November 1, 2007.

are available at most of these clinics, school policy prevents many from giving out contraceptives.

3. Interventions that include peer providers offer family planning and reproductive health services to teenagers. Their key attribute is that the non-medical portion of health visits are provided by teenagers themselves within a health care setting. These teenage "providers" are trained to offer such services as patient intakes, counseling about reproductive health and contraception, and outreach services. In this model, teenage and adult staff are treated equally and are offered similar training and compensation. Clients receive services in a confidential, non-judgmental environment that has been designed with teenagers in mind. The rationale behind peer provider models is

that teenagers may feel more comfortable talking about reproductive health issues with other teenagers and may be more likely to absorb and attend to these messages. In fact, some research has shown that peer health educators can be equally or more effective than adult educators.

Specific Clinic Protocols for Teens

Within any of these three basic models, special protocols for teens appear to improve teen contraceptive use. The list of characteristics of successful teen clinics that follows was created after examining the independent service components of the effective interventions found in the literature. None of the interventions that we reviewed contained all of the components listed below and, as mentioned earlier, the evaluations did not attempt to determine which specific components of the interventions provoked change in the participants. However, most of the protocol characteristics listed below have been described as important both in the literature on teen pregnancy prevention and in the evaluations of the successful interventions themselves.

A Wide Range of Services

Successful teen clinics provide their clients with:

Longer appointment times and individual counseling about the adolescent's own behavior. One common change that effective teen clinic interventions have employed is to increase counseling time or offer longer appointment times. This counseling often covers such topics as abstinence, contraceptive use, and the individual's own behavior. For example, the Self Center, a school-linked health clinic, offered in depth individual and group counseling to patients during certain hours of the day. Similarly, many clinic-based interventions have offered longer appointment times for teens to allow for individual counseling. A survey of public family planning agencies indicates that most routinely provide teenagers and adolescents with counseling about abstinence and talking to parents about sex.

Educational programs. Nearly half of public family planning clinics have put in place some sort of education program either on site or at other facilities that adolescents frequent. Many of these clinics have programs that focus on delaying sexual activity. A few of these agencies even provide incentives to encourage teenagers not to become pregnant. Many of the effective clinic-based interventions reviewed for this report offer supplemental resources, workshops or activities related to reproductive health for their teen patients. Some programs offered brochures and/or video or audiotaped programs as a part of regular office visits. Other clinic-based interventions offered supplemental workshops for their patients that met weekly for several weeks. These workshops often included role playing and skill building activities and they covered such topics as ways to reduce certain risks, abstinence, and condom use.

Wide range of services. Many family planning clinics provide more than just family planning services. Clients can often receive reproductive and family health services at these clinics as well. The location and focus of the clinic (e.g., school-based, family planning clinic, hospital) may have an impact on whether it is possible to make a wide range of medical services available for teens. School-based health centers, in particular, often offer a wide range of medical services and do not focus solely on reproductive health.

Confidentiality and Contraceptives

Confidential Services. Confidentiality is particularly important for teenagers and can have a large impact on teenagers' use of reproductive health services. A recent study of adolescent females found that 59 percent of teen girls under age 18 who were seeking services at a Planned Parenthood clinic would refuse family planning services and delay STI and HIV [AIDS virus] testing and treatment if their parents were informed that they were being prescribed oral contraceptives. Family PACT, a series of state funded clinics in California, was able to assure confidentiality to teen patients because by law, parental consent for these services was not necessary. Likewise, [researcher J.] Jemmott and colleagues (2005) evaluated an effective HIV risk reduction program for African-American and Latina girls that took place in an adolescent medicine clinic and that offered confidential reproductive health services to clients. The evaluation results indicated that the incidence of unprotected sex over the last ninety days was significantly lower for participants in the intervention. In addition, intervention participants reported fewer sex partners and had a lower incidence of STIs. Similarly, in an

For such issues as family planning and sexually transmitted infections, birth control clinic services can provide clinic-based or school-based interventions, as well as interventions by trained peer providers.

effort to tailor its intervention to the special needs of adolescents, one program made confidentiality a core component of its program. That intervention succeeded in increasing contraceptive use and reducing teen pregnancy. Most clinics that report data on confidential services indicate that parental consent is not required for their adolescent and teen patients to receive prescriptions for contraceptives.

Contraceptives. Even though many of the evaluations of clinic-based interventions did not specify whether contraceptives or prescriptions for contraceptives were offered on-site, it is the case that many clinics offer both services. For example, the clinics involved in Family PACT offered patients a choice of all U.S. FDA [Food and Drug Administration] approved methods of contraception. One intervention, tailored to the special needs of adolescents, offered patients a prescription for their contraceptive of choice as well as a follow up appointment six weeks later to provide counseling on any difficulties that the teen was having with their chosen contraceptive. Most school-based health centers are restricted by district policy from dispensing contraceptives and/or prescriptions for contraceptives on site. However, many of the school-based health centers, such as those in the Denver public schools, offer referrals for students to receive contraceptives off site.

Low Cost, Convenience, and Flexibility

Free or low cost services. Many of the clinic-based programs offer services to teens at little or no cost. For example, Family PACT, which was created by the California State Assembly, provided reproductive health services through public sector and private provider clinics to California residents (including teens) whose income was at or below 200% of the federal poverty level and who did not have access to these types of services through other means. In addition, teens' income was calculated independent of their parents' income level which increased the likelihood of eligibility. Similarly, an HIV risk reduction intervention for African-American and Latina adolescent women that took place in an adolescent medicine clinic offered free family planning services to teens. Finally, the Self Center, a school-linked health center, offered reproductive and contraceptive health care at no cost to junior and senior high school students. These programs were successful at reducing the frequency of unprotected sex, increasing contraceptive use, and reducing teen pregnancy rates. Although the specific role of free/low cost contraceptives in achieving these reductions was not determined, it is reasonable to conclude that it was part of the explanation.

Convenient services. Convenience should play a large part in determining where clinics that serve teens are located (e.g., in or near schools, in target neighborhoods) and in their hours of operation. Some of the most effective interventions provided special or extended hours to make their services more convenient for their teenage clients.

Flexible medical protocol. As a part of their comprehensive effort to make teens more comfortable during their clinic visits, one intervention spread the initial visit over two appointments spaced two weeks apart. During the first visit, the teen was counseled about contraception. During the second visit, the teen received a pelvic exam and any other needed medical services. This intervention increased contraceptive use and decreased teen pregnancy. Additional flexible medical protocols used in successful programs were the advance provision of emergency contraceptives and quick start for oral contraceptives.

Education about important reproductive health skills. Many interventions also taught patients specific skills such as how to correctly use a condom and how to negotiate with a partner about contraceptive use, how to avoid risky sexual encounters, and how to communicate with partners.

Referrals and Outreach

Referrals for needed services. Teens often have needs that cannot be met by a clinic, such as services for mental health or substance abuse. Many of the effective interventions such as Family

PACT and the Self Center provided referrals to their teen patients for those services. In addition, as a part of their intervention, ASSESS offered patients a brochure that contained community resources available to their patients.

Active outreach. Two of the major challenges faced by clinics that provide reproductive health services for teens are: (1) getting teenagers in the door and, (2) making sure the right services are offered. Based on this review of effective programs, there are several common sense things that clinics can do to improve in both areas. In order to reach teenagers who are most in need, clinics should pay attention to location, visibility, and outreach. Clinics should be located in areas that are convenient and accessible to the teens who are most at risk for teen pregnancy. Finding the right location, however, is not enough to get teens into the clinic. Clinics should be prepared to identify the teens at greatest risk in their communities and actively recruit them by advertising, forming partnerships with other organizations (e.g., schools, community centers), and asking for referrals. The clinic itself should be well marked and easily identifiable by teens on the street. Other practical suggestions include:

- Place a sign on the clinic that can be easily seen on the street,
- Maintain a presence at community events, and
- Invite teens to refer their peers to the clinic.

FIVE

Requiring Parental Consent for Birth Control Threatens Teens' Sexual Health

The Women's Health Partnership of Emory University

> Under Title X funding, youths under eighteen years old are
> lawfully permitted to use family planning services without
> parental consent in the United States, including confiden-
> tial access to birth control. The following viewpoint main-
> tains that attempts in recent years, especially in the state of
> Georgia, to require parental consent for birth control is
> counterproductive to preventing teen pregnancy. If it were
> required, studies demonstrate that some minors may post-
> pone or stop using family planning services and even forgo
> contraceptives or use the unreliable withdrawal method in-
> stead. The author of this viewpoint, Women's Health Part-
> nership, is a program from the Women's and Children's
> Center of the Emory University School of Public Health in
> Atlanta, Georgia.

Although minor[s'] access to contraception is a heavily debated topic, access for minors (under age 18) is currently
protected by state and federal law. Minors are legally able to access family planning services without parental consent in all 50

states and the District of Columbia. This right is protected by the requirements of Title X funding, the primary source of family planning funds in the United States, which protects access to confidential health care services without regard to age. There have been several attempts at the state level to challenge confidentiality for minors, yet no state has revoked minor rights of confidential access to contraceptives to date.

The predominant arguments for parental consent requirements stem from the view that parents should be aware and apprised of their children's behaviors. However, scientific evidence suggests that minors may actually delay seeking treatment and family planning services if parental consent is required.

Georgia Legislation

Proposed Georgia legislation, HB 526, aims to change definitions related to family planning in Chapter 7 of Title 49 of the official Georgia Code. The wording would be changed to: "*The agencies, employees of such agencies, or contractors of such agencies shall not provide any medical referral services, contraceptives, or birth control devices to an unemancipated minor unless such minor seeking the services is accompanied by a parent or guardian who shows proper identification and states that he or she is the lawful parent or guardian of such minor and that such parent or guardian has been notified that such services have been requested by the minor.*" This is a change from the current policy which requires Georgia agencies to provide contraceptives and birth control devices to any one who is requesting the service. As of the end of the 2007 Georgia legislative session, HB 526 passed one reading in the Georgia House of Representatives and was scheduled for a second reading in the House of the Georgia General Assembly. It is unknown if this bill will be revisited in the 2008 legislative session. [Editor's note: It was not.]

Contraception and Parental Consent Laws

According to the Georgia Family Planning Program (2006), 26% of all clients were under the age of 20 with 13% being under the age of 18. The racial breakdown of all clients is 47% black, 47% white, and 6% other. These numbers are consistent with the national data presented by the Office of Population affairs from fiscal year 2005.

Although there is no data on the numbers of minors in Georgia that already inform their parent/guardian in their decision to obtain contraceptives or the effect that mandatory parental consent may have in Georgia, there have been numerous national studies on the topic. A 2002 study published in the *Journal of the American Medical Association (JAMA)* on the effects of mandatory parental notification for minors to access

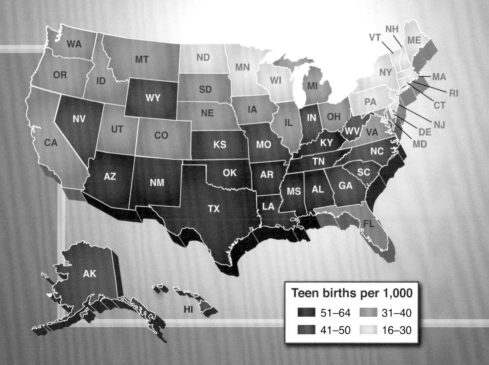

Teen Birthrates for Girls Aged Fifteen to Nineteen years, 2009

Teen birthrates were lowest in the Northeast and upper Midwest and highest across the southern states. These data come from the National Center for Health Statistics in 2009.

Teen births per 1,000

- 51–64
- 41–50
- 31–40
- 16–30

Taken from: Centers for Disease Control and Prevention, "Preventing Teen Pregnancy in the US," CDC Vital Signs, April 2011.

contraceptives found that 59% of respondents indicated they would either stop using family planning services, delay seeking care for HIV or sexually transmitted infections (STIs), or discontinue use of some services if parental notification were required. Although the survey was clear in stating that parental notification would only apply to contraception, eleven percent of participants indicated they would either delay or discontinue care for sexually transmitted infections as well.

A 2005 study published in *JAMA*, found that sixty percent of adolescent respondents reported that a parent/guardian knew they were seeking services at a family planning clinic. Fifty-nine percent of respondents reported they would use the clinic regardless of parental notification for prescription contraception. The response was dependent on whether the parent/guardian was already aware of the visit: among those who reported that their parent/guardian was unaware of their visit, thirty percent would continue seeking services, compared with seventy-nine percent of those that reported there was already parental knowledge of the visit. Of those who reported that parental knowledge would change their behavior, forty-six percent reported they would switch to an over-the-counter contraceptive method and eighteen percent would go to a private physician whom they believe would maintain confidentiality. Twenty percent of the respondents who reported likely behavior change in the case of required parental consent reported they would use no contraception or use the withdrawal method and only 1% indicated they would stop having sex.

Currently according to a national survey, minors wait an average of approximately 18 months after becoming sexually active to access family planning servicers. The studies provide information that mandatory parental notification for contraceptives will likely increase the amount of time that minors wait to access family planning services, if they access the services at all.

The Impact of Title X Funding

One of the largest effects of a mandatory parental consent law for minors to access contraception in Georgia would be the loss

A pregnancy counselor consoles a client watching a prenatal development video in a birth control clinic. A survey found that 59 percent of adolescents would obtain prescription contraception from such clinics with or without their parent's consent.

of Title X funding. Title X funds are federal funds for family planning services that, along with 10% matching state funds, are designated for family planning. Title X was created in 1970 in the Public Health Service Act and is administered through the Office of Population Affairs by the Office of Family Planning. This is the only federal program designated for family planning and related preventative healthcare and is aimed at providing care for low-income persons, regardless of sex, race, age, or ethnicity. As such, regulations for Title X funding mandate that confidential services must be provided for anyone who requests them, regardless of age or citizenship status. Without Title X funding a state is completely responsible for providing all family planning funding for its citizens. Title X funds currently provide the large majority of family planning funds in Georgia and other states.

Georgia currently receives $8.3 million from Title X funding and serves approximately 180,000 clients. In 2005, Georgia provided 158,145 STI tests, 79,459 breast exams, 77,529 pap smears, and 13,826 HIV tests to clients that may not have been able to obtain these services otherwise. Seventy-nine percent of Title X clients are either unemployed or the working poor and most are uninsured. Georgia currently ranks 9th in the nation for most births among teenagers, a statistic likely to worsen with parental consent laws or lack of Title X funding.

Without Title X funding, Georgia would expect to experience approximately 50,000 unplanned births annually by women who use the Georgia Family Planning Program (GFPP). Women with unintended pregnancies are less likely to seek timely prenatal care and more likely to have low birth-weight babies, which can cost up to $30,000 per month after delivery and are at risk for having life-long disabilities. According to the Family Planning Branch of the Georgia Department of Human Resources, every dollar spent on family planning services saves $4.40 on medical care, welfare, and nutritional programs for children under the age of 2. This could total a savings of $16 million over two years. Additionally, every dollar spent on family planning can save $3 in Medicaid costs for prenatal and newborn care.

Other States' Legislation

There is no state in the nation that has mandatory parental notification for minor access to contraception. Currently there are two states that have passed legislation that limit minor access to contraception. In 1997, the Texas legislature enacted a bill that prevents state funds from being used to provide contraceptives and medications to treat sexually transmitted infections to minors without parental consent. Utah passed a similar law that prevents state funds from being used to provide minors with contraception without parental consent. Neither of these laws restricts Title X funding and has, therefore, not been found unconstitutional.

New York. In 1997, the state of New York tried to ban the distribution of condoms to anyone under the age of 16. The legislation was struck down by the Supreme Court in *Carey v. Population Services International* (1977) on the premise that there was no medical reason for restricting minor access to contraceptives; rather that the legislation was a result of the state frowning upon early sexual behavior. The Supreme Court further noted that this legislation was lacking any evidence that supported that restricting access of minors to contraception would reduce sexual activity. This landmark ruling extended confidential family planning services, including birth control measures, to minors.

Utah. A similar ruling was made by the Federal District Courts in the case *Planned Parenthood Association of Utah v. Matheson* (1981). A Utah law requiring parental notification for distribution of contraceptives was found unconstitutional on the grounds that it conflicted with federal policy that encouraged providing contraceptives to minors that requested them. The Utah law was also found to infringe upon the rights of minors because it did not provide a method of distributing contraceptives to a mature minor or a minor whose best interests were at stake.

South Carolina. In 2000, the South Carolina House of Representatives passed a bill that prohibited the use of state funds to distribute contraceptives to minors under 16 if the parents objected. The legislation did not make it out of committee and the bill was never enacted.

Federal Legislative Attempts

In 1998 the U.S. House of Representatives passed legislation requiring parental notification for distribution of contraception to minors, but the Senate failed to pass the legislation and it was never enacted. No other federal legislative attempts at parental notification have managed to make it out of conference.

It is unknown if the issue of parental notification for contraceptive access for minors will be revisited in the 2008 Georgia legislative session. Notably, most debates on this topic focus on the appropriateness of sexual activity among teenagers and not on the larger impact of reducing access to contraception. Even beyond the very important issues of pregnancy and STIs for adolescents, enacting legislation that would remove Title X funding from the state of Georgia would have devastating effects on the ability to provide family planning and related healthcare services for all Georgians, regardless of age.

SIX

Not Requiring Parental Consent for Birth Control Places Youths at Risk

Ethan Bratt

Ethan Bratt is a marriage and family counselor in Colorado Springs, Colorado. In the following viewpoint Bratt opposes the 2007 decision of a Maine middle school to provide students access to birth control without parental consent. While favoring the availability of condoms, he maintains that preteens should obtain permission for birth control pills because of the health risks of hormonal contraception, such as lethal blood clots and potential emotional and developmental problems. Additionally, preteens lack the maturity and insight to wisely choose and use birth control pills, Bratt states, and parental consent is necessary to provide them guidance.

For those who haven't heard, on 10/17/2007, the Portland, Maine, School Committee just approved a proposal that allows students at Kind Middle School to be prescribed birth control. . . . It passed with a 7–2 vote.

Let me explain some of the details. First, this covers students in grades 6–8, which generally covers ages 11–13. It is only available to parents who have given permission for their children to be treated in the King Middle School's health center. There are no gradations of permission, meaning that if you give permission for your child to be treated for a sprained ankle they suffered during gym class or even Tylenol for a headache, you also have given permission for them to obtain birth control.

Originally, this was simply the distribution of condoms. As of the passage of the proposal it also means that 11-year-old girls will be able to go in and be examined by a physician or nurse practitioner and receive prescriptions for a full range of birth control. From [an article in the *Portland (ME) Press Herald*]: "Types of prescription birth control available through the health centers include contraceptive pills, patches or injections, as well as the morning-after pill. Diaphragms and IUDs [intrauterine devices] are not usually prescribed, [Lisa Belanger, a nurse practitioner who oversees the city's student health centers] said."

The Health Hazards

Now here's the kicker: as per Maine laws, children have a right to seek confidential health care, which means that the clinic is prohibited from telling the parents about any treatment the children receive. They encourage the children to tell their parents, but they cannot force the children to and the clinic cannot disclose it.

For starters, I am not opposed to the clinic making condoms available. At least in this matter, I am a realist and know that thanks to parents who are derelict in their responsibility to sexually educate their children and our grossly sexualized society, there are children who may choose to experiment sexually. Condoms are a barrier device and in addition to providing contraceptive measures, also protect against sexually transmitted diseases [STDs]. None of the current birth control measures protect against STDs. So strike one against them.

Secondly, there are the potential health hazards. Increased risks of cervical cancer, breast cancer, and lethal blood clots are all hazards. One 1997 study found that women who had previously used oral contraceptives were 40% more likely to have

Maine state representative Dale J. Crafts introduces a bill that would repeal Maine's current adult consent law. The bill would require notarized written consent of a parent or legal guardian before an abortion could be performed on a minor.

Lupus [erythematosus, a systemic autoimmune disease]. An increased incidence rate of all auto-immune diseases was found among pill users. On top of that, hormonal contraceptives can increase moodiness. With suicide being the third leading cause of death among young Americans and rates for suicide among

10-14 year-old-girls (exactly the age range we are talking about) up 76% from previous rates and teenage girl suicides up in general, do we need to potentially add to the problem with mood altering contraceptives? That is in addition to the increased likelihood of depression in teenage girls who are sexually active. With the exception of the diaphragm, which isn't even a commonly prescribed measure, all of those are hormone changing agents and in the case of some IUDs (intra-uterine devices: a device that is inserted into the [uterus] that do several things including plugging the fallopian tubes so that sperm cannot enter and fertilize the egg) they stop the menstrual cycle completely and the recipient no longer has periods! Recently, some oral contraceptives have also eliminated periods altogether. I am a bit out of my league in discussing the emotional and societal right of passage associated with menarche [the onset of menses], the stabilizing of the menstrual period, and how learning to handle the God-given gift of reproduction impacts a young teen girl, but I will venture a guess that taking a pill that stops all of that when it has barely started may have some long-term implications on a psycho-emotional level. . . .

Removing Parents from the Scenario

I guess the worst part of all this is the removal of the parents from the scenario. Suddenly, an 11-year-old is expected to be mature enough to make these decisions and deal with the ensuing consequences with no support from her parents. She is supposed to have the foresight, wisdom, and clarity of thought necessary to make what would be a decision that will have effects that echo for decades if not her entire life.

But, after all, who are we to tell our kids anything or to teach them anything. There is a quote attributed to [early twentieth-century US president] Theodore Roosevelt that goes: "To educate a man in mind and not in morals is to educate a menace to society." In today's society, this is laughed at and some people thoroughly disagree with it, questioning why we as parents have any right to teach our children what is right or wrong.

One such man is [former] Presidential hopeful John Edwards. Courtesy of *The Boston Globe* article "Don't leave educating our children to the government":

When the party's presidential candidates debated at Dartmouth College recently, they were asked about a controversial incident in Lexington, Mass., where a second-grade teacher, to the dismay of several parents, had read her young students a story celebrating same-sex marriage. Were the candidates "comfortable" with that?

"Yes, absolutely," former senator John Edwards promptly replied. "I want my children . . . to be exposed to all the information . . . even in second grade . . . because I don't

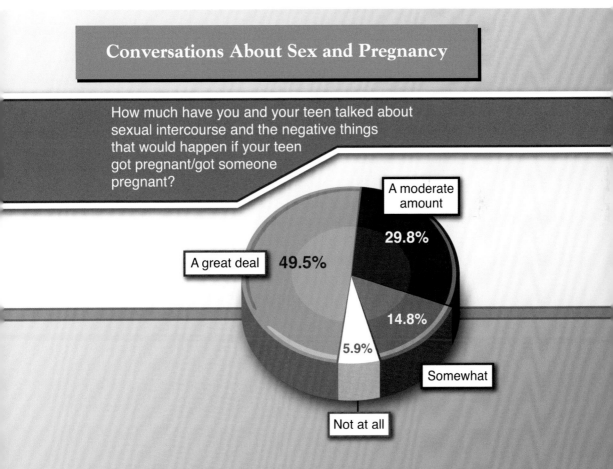

Conversations About Sex and Pregnancy

How much have you and your teen talked about sexual intercourse and the negative things that would happen if your teen got pregnant/got someone pregnant?

A moderate amount
29.8%

A great deal 49.5%

14.8%

5.9%

Somewhat

Not at all

want to impose my view. Nobody made me God. I don't get to decide on behalf of my family or my children. . . . I don't get to impose on them what it is that I believe is right."

Sadly, Mr. Edwards, it is looking like the option of teaching our kids and helping to guide them is being legislated right out of parents' hands. I recognize why the law prohibiting clinics from disclosing information to parents exists. It is to protect that minority of children whose parents are abusive or neglectful from retaliating against them should the child seek treatment for an abuse injury or turn to an adult for help with a medical problem that, for whatever reason, they cannot turn to their parents for. But instead of penalizing all parents and leaving them in the dark, couldn't a way be devised to only penalize the bad ones? An example from off the top of my head, if children feel that their parents will be abusive or retaliate against them, they can opt to have it kept confidential and then turn the case over to a social worker for follow up.

I don't know what the answer is, but I know that Maine laws and the laws in so many other states that make a blanket abridgment of all parents' rights are not.

SEVEN

Teens Must Use Birth Control in Serious Relationships

Melissa Daly

In the following selection writer Melissa Daly discusses the need for teens to use birth control in serious relationships. Even if the couple is genuinely in love, their readiness for sex is a different issue, she explains. Love may create a sense of trust and emotional intimacy—influencing couples to discontinue the use of condoms and other contraceptives—but it also blinds them to the faults of their partners and does not protect against pregnancy or sexually transmitted infections. The author provides a checklist of sexual health and birth control for young couples to follow before deciding to have sex.

"It's OK if you're in love." That's what some teens say about having sex. On the other hand, some teens don't feel the need to love or even be in a relationship with their partners to get physical. "There's no one common belief among teens today about any aspect of sex and love," remarks Benedict W., 17, a member of the Washington, D.C., Teen Advisory Group of the National Campaign to Prevent Teen and Unplanned Pregnancy. "Although, love is often seen as a complication," she adds, such as when one partner feels it and the other doesn't.

"Perhaps you should be in love before you have sex with someone," but love alone isn't enough of a reason, says Karen

Rayne, a sex educator in Austin, Texas. "'Are you in love or not' is something important to ponder, but 'should you have sex or not' is a very different kind of question." So how do you figure out whether you are really in love—and what does that mean about your readiness for sex?

Crazy in Love

Love means different things to different people. To some, it's that butterflies-in-the-stomach feeling at the beginning of a new romance. For others, it's the long-term attachment that comes way after the butterflies in a committed relationship. For many research scientists studying love, it's both.

Almost everyone, however, can agree that lust is another animal. The hormone testosterone (which everyone has) kicks into gear during adolescence, making it possible to desire a physical connection without any interest in an emotional one. That desire is lust, or physical attraction—a result of the natural human sex drive. It might come as a feeling of "love at first sight," or even a sexual arousal reflex such as an erection or vaginal lubrication. If you list the things you like about a potential partner and they're all physical attributes, such as great hair or a nice body, lust is most likely what you're feeling. The fluttery, flushed feeling you get around a crush may be similar to the excitement of a new love, but if you don't actually know much about each other's personalities, it's probably still lust for the moment. Of course, lust can grow into love, but it doesn't always.

When one partner is in love and the other only in lust, having sex can make a subsequent rejection more painful. Of course, even being mutually in love is no magic charm against heartbreak. However, the longer you spend together and the better you get to know each other, the more solid your bond may become. "I call it 'dating through the seasons,'" says Nancy Brown, an adolescent relationship and sexuality expert and education project manager at Palo Alto Medical Foundation in California. "Most of us can be on our best behavior for a while, but we start letting down our guard by about three to four months." After that point, you'll see more sides of your partners—such as how she or he handles bad days or conflicts—rather than just the perfect image that person displays at first. Going through those times together could bring you closer or make you realize that you and the other person might not be the best match after all.

One more way to evaluate the depth of your relationship is to ask your best friend what he or she thinks about the object of your affection. "Often when you're in love, you don't have a good sense of the person. You have a warm, fuzzy feeling, but that's not the same as a cold, hard look at him or her—and it's not supposed to be," says Rayne. "Your friends are much more

According to the author, teen couples genuinely in love may have a level of trust and emotional intimacy that causes them to stop using contraceptives.

able to be objective and say whether they're feeling that same warmth about him or her." If they aren't, you don't have to break up. Just put the brakes on sex for six months, let everyone get to know one another more, and see how things look later.

Love Is Blind

In the midst of a new romance, you're really not thinking straight. And that's where the intertwining of lust and love can be a problem. When you're in love, your significant other can do no wrong in your eyes—your feelings for him or her are so overpowering that you can't imagine she or he would hurt you, even unintentionally. That sense of trust, and also concern over what your partner will think of you, may be why teens are less likely to use condoms when hooking up with a serious relationship partner than with a casual partner, according to a recent study in the *Journal of Adolescent Health*. "No matter how deeply in love you are, it's not protecting your cervix or your penis from bacteria and viruses," says Brown. "Love is no guarantee against pregnancy, disease, or even sometimes a partner's infidelity." Sexual activity with anyone carries serious risks, including unplanned pregnancy and sexually transmitted infections (STIs).

Love and sex need to stay separate in your mind at least long enough to arrange for—and use—protection, says Brown. That means condoms to reduce the transmission of STIs, plus, for vaginal intercourse, a backup contraceptive method such as the birth control pill, patch, or ring. While love itself doesn't make sex safer, it can create a more favorable environment for healthy sexuality. "If your partner really loves you, he or she will go with you to the clinic a month beforehand to get protection, use it, and be committed to making sure you have a good experience," says Brown. "If not, his or her motivations may not be the same as yours."

Having multiple sexual partners—either sleeping with several different people or having a series of exclusive relationships—increases the risk of STIs. Any sort of limiting criteria—such as having sex only with someone a person loves, or is in a long-term, committed relationship with, or is married to—helps reduce the chances of contracting an infection.

What Is a Healthy Relationship?

Just as love doesn't make you immune from infections, neither does it ensure you're in a healthy relationship. That can make a big difference in whether sex is a positive or a negative experience. People often say that communication is the key to a good relationships—but what does that really mean?

"I give teens a list of 10 things to do before they have sex, many of which require a conversation with their partner," says Rayne. "If they can manage to go through each item on their own, then talk about each one together, that indicates they have

Teens' Opinions on How Important It Is to Be in Love Before Having Sexual Intercourse

Do not know
1%

Not important at all
3%

Not too important
9%

Very important
68%

Somewhat important
23%

Taken from: Princeton Survey Research Associates International, NBC News, *People Magazine.* "National Survey of Young Teens Sexual Attitudes and Behaviors," 2004.

good communication." Cruising through them solo isn't enough, she adds. "A big part of being in a healthy sexual relationship is reciprocity—that is, making sure each partner is giving and taking in approximately equal amounts." Here is that list of 10 things to do:

1. *Know each other's sexual history.* This is about more than just determining your partner's disease risk. "It's about getting to know where your partner is coming from, how well they know themselves, how responsible they've been, which can tell you a lot about a person," says Rayne.

2. *Know your partner's STI status and your own.* Get tested before you have sex—even if neither partner has had sex before. Call it a trial run.

3. *Discuss exactly what birth control and STI protection you'll use.* Both partners should be involved in the decision.

4. *For heterosexual couples, discuss what you'll do if the woman gets pregnant.* Agree on a hypothetical plan, acknowledging that your feelings could change if it actually happened.

5. *Get your best friend's blessing.* Having a second opinion helps.

6. *Meet your partner's parents.* It'll help you know him or her more deeply—even if he or she is nothing like the family.

7. *Learn what turns you on.* Know what does and doesn't feel good to you so you're able to show your partner.

8. *Be comfortable naked in front of each other.* If that sounds crazy, it's totally understandable—but it may mean you're not ready for sex yet.

9. *Have protection ready.* Even if you are both certified infection-free and monogamous, using it is just a good habit to start and maintain.

10. *Make sure your partner does each of these things too.* Take care of yourself and each other.

Remember: Checking off each item on a list doesn't automatically mean it's the right time for you to have sex. The same goes for being in love. Putting both your head and your heart into every new sexual decision is the surest way to wind up happy with the choices you've made.

EIGHT

Teens Use Condoms More Consistently than Adults Do

Stephen Smith

Adolescents are perceived to be reckless and oblivious to the consequences of their actions; however, Stephen Smith, a staff writer for the *Boston Globe*, suggests that the use of condoms is more widespread among teenagers than it is among adults. According to a recent national study, about 79 percent of fourteen- to seventeen-year-old sexually active males used condoms the last time they had intercourse; eighteen- to twenty-four-year olds were half as likely to use condoms in comparison. Smith continues that this safety precaution declines even more as adults enter their fifties; at this age, adults use condoms less than one-third of the time. In fact, talking about sexual practices and condoms with the middle aged presents its own issues and difficulties, Smith notes.

It is the age of invincibility: adolescence, when the thrill of the moment is unperturbed by the consequences of the future. Except, maybe, when it comes to sex. Two recent studies—one, a national survey; the other, a report from Boston health trackers —found widespread use of condoms among the nearly one-third of adolescents who had intercourse, belying the portrayals of wanton recklessness that are the coin of the cable [TV] realm.

This is a generation whose entire lifetime has been framed by the presence of the AIDS virus. So, some sex researchers aver, teens today are keenly aware of the importance of condoms (although there's also evidence that certain sexually transmitted diseases are rising among youths, complicating the analysis).

And, it turns out, they might have a thing or two they could teach their parents or grandparents. The same national survey found that adults in their 40s, 50s, and 60s who were still playing on the field of love—they described their intimates as "casual partners" as opposed to "relationship partners"—used protection at substantially lower levels than youngsters.

Maybe they should listen to Anastasia Walker, a take-no-prisoners 17-year-old who starred a couple of years back in an online video touting the virtues of safe sex.

Teens' Familiarity with Birth Control

Percent responding *a lot* or *somewhat* familiar

Birth Control Method	Total 15–17	Gender	
		Boys	Girls
Condoms	85	87	83
Female Condoms	35	37	32
A Diaphragm	35	32	38
A Cervical Cap	18	13	23
An Intrauterine Device (IUD)	12	8	15
The Shot, or Depo-Provera	40	26	55
The Patch	61	53	69
The Ring	21	15	26
The Pill	77	73	82

Taken from: Kaiser Family Foundation and *Seventeen*. "Birth Control and Protection." *Sex Smarts*, July 2004.

"A lot of people know someone who got something on the down low," said Walker, a junior at TechBoston Academy. "So you're like, 'Wow, I don't want to be like that.' So I know a lot of teenagers who always do use condoms."

The countrywide data documenting condom use—the participants spanned the ages, as young as 14, as old as 94—are part of a series of studies depicting love, American style, circa the 21st century. The lead authors of the research, published in the *Journal of Sexual Medicine*, are the intellectual progeny of Alfred Kinsey, the bow-tied biologist who began his academic life studying wasps and concluded it exploring the sexual proclivities of humans.

The National Survey of Sexual Health and Behavior underwritten by the maker of Trojan brand condoms, depicts the vibrant, varied sexual life of Americans—and its durability, even deep into life, with people in their 70s and beyond craving physical connection.

"The easiest thing you could conclude from this is that sex is practiced at all ages, from very young to very, very old," said Dr. Irwin Goldstein, director of San Diego Sexual Medicine, who was not involved in the study. "It's a reality of human life at all levels, at all times of life.

"As I personally start to age and get into my 60s," he said, "it's nice to see they have data showing sex is widely practiced in both men and women at older ages."

It is the findings about condom use that sparked the most interest among researchers in human sexuality—both because they suggest what's working and what more needs to be done.

Adolescent Condom Use Is Rising

Condom use among adolescents has been rising in recent years, and the rates reported in the national study from researchers at Indiana University—they surveyed nearly 6,000 adults and adolescents—stand as some of the highest ever recorded.

About 79 percent of sexually active males between 14 and 17 said they used condoms during their most recent sexual encounter; that compares with 65 percent of 15- to 19-year-olds in a 2001 federal study.

WOODSON

A Boston Public Health Commission study reported similar patterns: Among sexually active Boston high school students, 73 percent said they used protection during their most recent sex act.

And just last week [in February 2011] a federal health agency reported that the nation's teen birth rate had fallen to a historic low—another potential piece of evidence that adolescents are using protection.

"We often as a country make the assumption that adolescents are sort of being risky and irresponsible and promiscuous," said a leader of the national survey on sexuality, Michael Reece, director of the Center for Sexual Health Promotion at Indiana University. "To be at a point where adolescents are using condoms at a high rate, that's a monumental change in how we think about sexuality."

It would be incorrect, though, to conclude that the majority of adolescents are having sex with abandon. In fact, the study found that not even a third of adolescents had engaged in intercourse by the time they reached 17.

Still, those findings emerge at a time when disease detectives are sounding alarms about rising diagnoses of chlamydia, among the most common sexually transmitted diseases. In Boston, for example, teen chlamydia cases climbed 70 percent from 1999 to 2008, with about 24 cases per 1,000 youths.

Further complicating the story, it's unclear how much of that increase is actually attributable to improved testing techniques and expanded screening campaigns for a disease that often lingers silently before, in rare cases, causing infertility.

Cindy Engler, director of child and adolescent health services at Boston's hearth agency, said it's clear to her that some students may hear the admonishments to use condoms but fail to do so. What's less clear, she said, is why. One possible reason: "When you're talking about adolescents," Engler said, "it's a lot more challenging to negotiate with your partner about the use of a condom."

Walker, the Boston teen, said that while condom use appears to be standard practice among her peers, she suspects some youths shade the truth when answering surveys.

A recent national study reported that 79 percent of sexually active boys aged fourteen to seventeen used a condom the last time they had intercourse, while youth eighteen to twenty-four had been half as likely to use condoms.

"I do know people who lie about using a condom so they won't be embarrassed," she said, "and so that people won't look at them like they're nasty."

A Cautionary Tale

There's no denying this: Condom use plummets as adolescence fades into young adulthood. The national study found that 18- to 24-year-old men who engaged in casual encounters were about half as likely to use condoms as adolescent males. The authors of the study called for reinvigorated education measures emphasizing the importance of protection as youths enter adulthood—and beyond.

By the time people reach their 50s, protection practices decline even further, with both men and women who are in casual relationships reporting they use condoms far less than one-third of the time.

That should serve as a cautionary tale, said Kevin Fenton, director of the US Centers for Disease Control and Prevention branch that oversees efforts to slow sexually transmitted infections, known as STIs. "Although the majority of STIs and HIV are seen in individuals under age 40," Fenton said, "increasingly we're seeing STI and HIV [the AIDS virus] among older populations."

Persuading the middle-aged to discuss their sexual practices —and even be tested for infections—proves daunting, said another author of the national study, Debby Herbenick.

"For many people in their 50s, 60s, 70s, and beyond, the idea of asking about STI testing may make you feel like you've done something wrong or you've been promiscuous or that people will think you picked a partner who's been unfaithful to you—all that shame and stigma," Herbenick said.

In his practice at Boston Medical Center, certified sex therapist Stanley Ducharme sees patients from 18 to 80. To his older patients, condoms are a latex method to prevent pregnancy, not stanch infectious diseases.

"Whether they're a widower or divorced, I don't think they see the importance or the necessity of using a condom," Ducharme said. "So I think we could say young people have something to teach in terms of protecting themselves."

NINE

Teens Who Do Not Use Condoms Fear Disapproval from Partners

AIDS Alert

The journal *AIDS Alert* contends in the following article that disapproval from sexual partners discourages some adolescents from using condoms. In a survey of fifteen- to twenty-one-year-olds, two-thirds did not use one the last time they had sex, expressing concerns of partner disapproval and less sexual pleasure. And respondents indicated that they were less likely to discuss condom use with their partners. Other reasons and beliefs described by experts include that condoms are a hassle, that not using one is a sign of commitment, that condoms provoke suspicion from partners, and that they break easily. In conclusion, *AIDS Alert* maintains that comprehensive sex education can address the fears adolescents have of condoms.

A survey of more than 1,400 adolescents and young adults indicates that teens who don't use condoms were significantly more likely to believe that condoms reduce sexual pleasure and also were more concerned that their partner would not approve of condom use.

In addition, a separate study found that adolescents might not be getting the information they need when it comes to condom use and negotiation skills. Commonly used abstinence-only curricula don't provide complete, current, or accurate medical knowledge about the effectiveness of condoms, states a 2008 review of current programs.

The three programs assessed were Me, My World, My Future (published by Teen-Aid for use by middle school students), Sexuality, Commitment & Family (published by Teen-Aid for use by high school students), and Why kNOw (published by AAA Women's Services for sixth grade through high school). They often provide inaccurate medical information to adolescents, and this information includes false or misleading statements about the effectiveness and safety of condoms, the review says. The programs inflate the actual failure rate of condoms, which suggests that using condoms is somewhat like playing "Russian roulette" with HIV, the report notes.

To understand teens' use of condoms, investigators from the Bradley Hasbro Children's Research Center in Providence, RI, and three other institutions surveyed more than 1,400 adolescents and young adults between the ages of 15 and 21 who had unprotected sex in the previous 90 days.

Study participants in Atlanta, Miami, and Providence completed an audio computer-assisted interview to gather information about sexual risk behaviors including condom use. Questions included attitudes and perceptions about condom use, and communication and negotiation with partners about condom use. The study group included 797 females and 613 males. About half were African American. Almost one-fourth (24%) were Hispanic, and 19% were white.

Researchers found that two-thirds of adolescents did not use a condom the last time they had sex. Participants also reported an average of two partners and about 15 incidents of unprotected sexual activity within the 90-day period. In addition to concerns about reduced sexual pleasure and partner disapproval, teens who did not use condoms also were less likely to discuss condom use with their partners. Those findings held true across racial/ethnic groups, gender, and geographic locations, researchers report.

"It's clear that we have to address these attitudes, fears, and concerns that many teens have regarding condom use, if we want to reduce their risk for contracting a sexually transmitted infection," says Larry Brown, MD, professor in the Department of Psychiatry and Human Behavior in the Alpert School of Medicine at Brown University. "The good news is that these attitudes may be easily influenced and changed through clinical and community-based interventions."

A recent survey of individuals aged fifteen to twenty-one revealed that two-thirds of them did not use condoms the last time they had sex, concerned that their partner would disapprove or have less sexual pleasure.

The Rising Use of First-Time Contraception

Percentage of women aged fifteen to forty-four years who used a method of contraception at their first premarital intercourse: United States, 2006–2008.

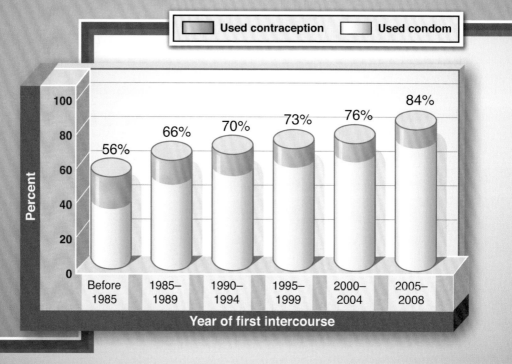

Taken from: W.D. Mosher and J. Jones. "Use of Contraception in the United States: 1982–2008." *Vital and Health Statistics*, 2010, pp. 23, 29.

What Influences Condom Use?

What are some of the most common attitudes and concerns influencing condom use in adolescents? Consider these possibilities, says Brown, who served as lead author for the current research:

- Teens might have negative feelings about personal factors about condoms. They might see donning a condom as a hassle, something that will ruin the mood of sex, and make sex less pleasurable.
- Teens worry that their partners won't want to use condoms, says Brown. They might be suspicious about the reason for

using a condom, or they might want to not use one as a sign of commitment.

- Teens might not use condoms when they have difficulty talking with their partners about condom use in the role of safer sex. Adolescents might not feel that they are able to refuse or delay sex until it is safer, says Brown.

"Two other reasons teenagers and older couples don't use condoms is that they think condoms don't work; one reason why they think that they don't work is because they frequently break," says Robert Hatcher, MD, MPH, professor of gynecology and obstetrics at Emory University School of Medicine in Atlanta. "When used, condoms are effective in preventing both infection and pregnancy, and when used correctly, condoms break only 1% to 2% of the time."

What are some specific ways that health care providers can address those attitudes and concerns? Screen teens' sexual behavior, says Brown. Discuss whether they are having sex and whether condoms are used at all and with all partners. If consistent condom use is not in play, discuss what barriers impede such use.

Teach teens how to bring up discussions of sex and condoms in a mutually caring, respectful, and tactful manner, says Brown. Counsel that most partners won't refuse with this approach, he notes.

Reduce teens' discomfort with condoms by encouraging them to continue to try condoms and finding a brand that provides optimal fit, comfort, and sensation. Condom makers now are making condom use more pleasurable with freshening wipes, lubricants, ribbings, and even vibrating rings, reports Anita Nelson, MD, professor in the Obstetrics and Gynecology Department at the David Geffen School of Medicine at the University of California in Los Angeles.

Refer teens to small group interventions with other teens, such as those offered at community-based organizations, that address those issues, offers Brown.

Continue to provide comprehensive sexuality education [which promotes birth control methods as well as abstinence] to adolescent patients, especially if your state accepts abstinence-only sexuality education funds. As of August 2008, the following states had opted out of Title V abstinence-only federal funding: Alaska, Arizona, California, Colorado, Connecticut, Delaware, District of Columbia, Idaho, Iowa, Maine, Massachusetts, Minnesota, New Jersey, New Mexico, New York, Ohio, Pennsylvania, Rhode Island, Tennessee, Vermont, Virginia, Washington, Wisconsin, and Wyoming.

States that have rejected federal abstinence-only funds generally cite concerns about the efficacy and accuracy of abstinence-only curricula. Those states also tend to have progressive governments and strong advocates for comprehensive sexuality education, notes an overview of state trends.

TEN

Morning-After Pills Should Be Accessible to Teens

Heather Corinna

In 2006 the Food and Drug Administration (FDA) approved the sale of the emergency contraception pill Plan B without a prescription at pharmacies for women eighteen and over. Three years later, the FDA expanded access to Plan B to minors seventeen and older without a prescription and sixteen and younger with a prescription. In the following viewpoint written in 2006 when Plan B was only available to women eighteen and older, Heather Corinna, an activist and founder of Scarleteen, a sex education website for teens, argues that the pill should also be accessible over-the-counter to all women of reproductive age, including minors. More than eight hundred thousand teenagers become pregnant in the United States each year, she reports, with many opting for abortion. Restricting the over-the-counter dispensing of Plan B to those eighteen and over is a missed opportunity to prevent unplanned pregnancies, Corinna states. She also gives advice on what individuals should do if a pharmacist refuses to sell emergency contraception to women of legal age.

The morning after pill is now legal in the U.S. for over-the-counter use, without a prescription, for those over 18. But what does that mean to you [if you are under eighteen]?

Following is an in-depth question and answer page about the decision [as it was first rendered in 2006, for women eighteen and over] and how it is applied for all women, about Plan B, and about pharmacist refusals and how to manage them.

The FDA [Food and Drug Administration] press release from the day of the decision, in September of 2006, stated:

> The U.S. Food and Drug Administration (FDA) today announced approval of Plan B, a contraceptive drug, as an over-the-counter (OTC) option for women aged 18 and older. Plan B is often referred to as emergency contraception or the "morning after pill." It contains an ingredient used in prescription birth control pills—only in the case of Plan B, each pill contains a higher dose and the product has a different dosing regimen. Like other birth control pills, Plan B has been available to all women as a prescription drug. When used as directed, Plan B effectively and safely prevents pregnancy. Plan B will remain available as a prescription-only product for women age 17 and under.
>
> Duramed, a subsidiary of Barr Pharmaceuticals, will make Plan B available with a rigorous labeling, packaging, education, distribution and monitoring program. In the CARE (Convenient Access, Responsible Education) program Duramed commits to:
>
> • Provide consumers and healthcare professionals with labeling and education about the appropriate use of prescription and OTC Plan B, including an informational toll-free number for questions about Plan B;
>
> • Ensure that distribution of Plan B will only be through licensed drug wholesalers, retail operations with pharmacy services, and clinics with licensed healthcare practitioners, and not through convenience stores or other retail outlets where it could be made available to younger women without a prescription;

- Packaging designed to hold both OTC and prescription Plan B. Plan B will be stocked by pharmacies behind the counter because it cannot be dispensed without a prescription or proof of age; and

- Monitor the effectiveness of the age restriction and the safe distribution of OTC Plan B to consumers 18 and above and prescription Plan B to women under 18.

What Is Plan B?

Is Plan B just on the shelf like aspirin? No. Plan B/the Morning After Pill (MAP) will be kept behind the counter in pharmacies,

A doctor consults with a patient on the use of the morning-after pill. Many feel this pill should be made available over the counter to all women of reproductive age.

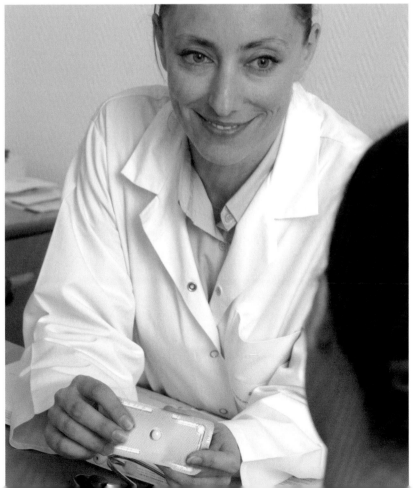

and a consumer purchasing it will be required to provide valid identification showing they are over the age of 18. Those under the age of 18 will still need a prescription to obtain Plan B. [Editor's note: In 2009 the FDA made Plan B available to seventeen-year-olds without a prescription and to females sixteen and under with a prescription.]

What will it cost? Barr Pharmaceuticals has stated that the current cost—around $25–$40—will likely increase for over the counter sales and for Plan B obtained by prescription, largely due to packaging changes. They have not stated by how much. For those who are insured or on Medicaid, they will likely be able to have most of their costs of EC (emergency contraception) covered with a small copayment for the medication.

Can someone over 18 legally get it for someone under 18? The FDA heads have compared sales of Plan B to the way sales of alcohol, cigarettes and nicotine replacement products go (we know, it's crazy to treat birth control as contraband: boy, do we know). However, at this time, there is no reason to assume that someone over 18 cannot practically and lawfully obtain EC for someone under 18.

The Princeton Emergency Contraception site has just added the following to their informational page on over-the-counter EC status: "Dr. [Steven] Galson said that the FDA is not in the business of regulating the practice of medicine or individual people's behavior as regards drug use. There are no restrictions against a person 18 or older buying the product in advance to have on hand for future use. There are no restrictions against a person 18 or older buying multiple packages of Plan B at one time. Opponents of the age restriction have noted that it will be much easier for young women to get an older friend or relative to buy Plan B for them than to get a doctor's prescription (and cheaper, too)."

How does Plan B work again? Is it abortion? Plan B is *contraception* (birth control). It works just like other methods of contraception do, by preventing pregnancy. The morning-after pill does not have the capacity to terminate an existing pregnancy, only to prevent one: it will not work if a woman has already become pregnant. While some who would like to keep women from being able to access Plan B have stated it resembles abortion, this is an untruth. Even the information from the FDA's press information on this change in Plan B status makes clear that is it contraception:

Plan B works like other birth control pills to prevent pregnancy. Plan B acts primarily by stopping the release of an egg from the ovary (ovulation). It may prevent the union of sperm and egg (fertilization). If fertilization does occur, Plan B may prevent a fertilized egg from attaching to the womb (implantation). If a fertilized egg is implanted prior to taking Plan B, Plan B will not work.

In case this is unclear, remember that pregnancy is not instantaneous: it does not occur immediately after a risk, but takes around 6–8 days to occur, which is why EC can work as it does to prevent pregnancy.

Plan B needs to be taken within 120 hours of a risk, and the sooner it is taken, the greater its effectiveness is. So, ideally, you will want to obtain EC if you need it as soon as you know you have had a risk. It can be helpful, for this reason, to either purchase Plan B over-the-counter if you are 18 and up in advance, or to ask your doctor or gynecologist for a prescription to fill, just to have on hand in case of a risk/birth control failure.

If you suspect you are pregnant, Plan B will *not* work to terminate a pregnancy. Unfortunately, some of those opposed to Plan B who have tried to intentionally misrepresent it, stating it is abortion, have achieved their end in some respects by confusing an awful lot of women.

If you wish to terminate a pregnancy, given the limited time window in which a termination can be done, it is useless to try and use Plan B/The MAP in hopes it will be a cheaper, easier way to do so. It cannot accomplish this end. If you suspect you are pregnant and think or know you may wish to terminate, you need to speak to an abortion provider about medical or surgical abortion.

Objections to the Age Limit

Will it ever be available over the counter to women under 18 in the States? We sure hope so, and Scarleteen as an organization strongly feels it *should* be available to women of reproductive age under 18. We feel the only reason it is not is not due to medical or practical concerns, but to political agendas and a strong desire for those in power to control women's lives, and usurp women's rights to ownership of their/our own bodies.

It is [available] in other countries, and obstetricians and gynecologists support that there is *no* medical or practical reason we currently know of which would provide sound cause *not* to provide EC over the counter for women not yet 18. In fact, the American College of Obstetricians and Gynecologists very directly expressed strong objections to the age limit in this statement here, in which they said,

> In light of the US Food and Drug Administration's (FDA) decision to approve over-the-counter (OTC) status for Plan B—emergency contraception (EC) for women age 18 and older, The American College of Obstetricians and Gynecologists (ACOG) today emphasized the need for unimpeded access to EC for all women of reproductive age. Timely access to emergency contraception is pivotal in reducing the number of unintended pregnancies and abortions in the US. By restricting its OTC availability to women age 18 and older, the FDA has missed an unparalleled opportunity to prevent teenage pregnancies. Each year there are more than 800,000 teen pregnancies in the US, with many ending in abortion. Pregnancy itself is not without risk, especially for a young woman. There is no scientific or medical reason to impose an age restriction and to withhold EC from this population. EC is safe for over-the-counter use by women of all ages.

The Kaiser Network's report on recent developments with EC access adds that the "Center for Reproductive Rights [CRR] lead attorney Simon Heller said the group will continue with its lawsuit against FDA over its rejection of Barr's first application for nonprescription Plan B sales, the Tribune reports. CRR—on behalf of the Association of Reproductive Health Professionals, the National Latina for

Reproductive Health and others—filed the suit in a U.S. District Court in New York, claiming the agency did not follow procedure when it denied the original nonprescription Plan B application. In a deposition in the case, John Jenkins, director of FDA's Office of New Drugs, said that Galson told him "that he felt he didn't have a choice" but to reject Barr's original application. Jenkins added that Galson "characterized that in a sense that he wasn't sure that he would be allowed to remain as center director if he didn't agree with the action". Heller said that CRR will seek to have the age restriction for nonprescription Plan B sales overturned through the lawsuit."

The FDA stated its reasons for not making it available over-the-counter to women under 18 so to be these: "because 1) adequate data were not provided to support a conclusion that young adolescent women can safely use Plan B for emergency contraception without the professional supervision of a licensed practitioner and 2) a proposal from the sponsor to change the requested indication to allow for marketing of Plan B as a prescription-only product for women under 16 years of age and a nonprescription product for women 16 years and older was incomplete and inadequate for a full review. Therefore, FDA concluded that the application was not approvable.

Given that there is no difference between women's bodies in general at the age of 18 and the age of 17 (though for two given women at that age, or at 18 and 21, for that matter, their development may differ), and given the FDA already found that it could be safe to sell to those 17 and older, with continued lobbying, this may not be all that challenging to refute and disprove. Data from other countries on long-term effects of Plan B for adolescent women who have been using it OTC for some time may be of use in doing this, as that data is available, and thus far, there is nothing to my knowledge which shows ill effects of Plan B in women under 18 as a whole. Undoubtedly, *some* age limit will be put on this even if the age limit is changed, which may be sound, given that in women of considerably younger ages, it's not unsound to presume that EC, like other hormonal medications, may have side effects in far younger women which would not be as prevalent in older teens and adult women.

FDA Commissioner [Andrew von] Eschenbach listed some other reasons in his own memo for making the age 18, such as that since 18 is the legal age for purchasing cigarettes, it would be easiest for pharmacists to remember. This and other "management issues" are being argued against, for obvious reasons.

If Pharmacists Refuse to Sell Plan B

So, a woman over 18 can just get it anywhere? Ideally, yes: a woman over 18 should be able to get Plan B at any pharmacy.

The big issue is that right now, there is a giant fracas among some pharmacists, the states they work in, and the pharmacy boards of each state about whether or not a pharmacist has the right to refuse to sell Plan B, both over the counter and when sold by prescription. Some pharmacists state that they morally object to Plan B because they consider it to be abortion, or "too close" to abortion, even though it works the same way birth control pills and other methods of contraception work; even though Plan B cannot terminate a pregnancy.

In April of 2005, a bill was put forth to Congress which would lawfully allow pharmacists in the US—despite the conflicts with the state board codes pharmacists are to adhere to via the refusals, which are generally only to occur if and when a pharmacist feels a medication may cause potential *physical* harm to a patient, such as via dangerous drug interactions or dosage errors—to "refuse to fill valid prescriptions for drugs or devices on the basis of personal beliefs, and for other purposes," called the Access to Legal Pharmaceuticals Act.

The congressional findings were that:

(1) An individual's right to religious belief and worship is a protected, fundamental right in the United States.

(2) An individual's right to access legal contraception is a protected, fundamental right in the United States.

(3) An individual's right to religious belief and worship cannot impede an individual's access to legal prescriptions, including contraception.

This resolved with the decision that if a given pharmacist refused to fill a prescription or provide an over-the-counter drug, that another pharmacist must provide it. If the product is not in stock, or a pharmacist refuses to stock it, the pharmacy must have another pharmacist order and supply the product. A penalty of $5,000 per day of violation. However, different states have different laws.

As well, the National Women's Law Center [NWLC] reports that,

The American Pharmacists Association (APhA) states: APhA recognizes the individual pharmacist's right to exercise conscientious refusal and supports the establishment of systems to ensure patient's access to legally prescribed therapy without compromising the pharmacist's right of conscientious refusal.

This policy has been interpreted by the APhA to require a pharmacist to refer to another pharmacist a prescription that he or she refuses to fill on grounds of conscience. The organization notes that the patient should not have any awareness that the pharmacist was refusing to fill the prescription. When the profession's policy is implemented correctly—and proactively—it is seamless to the patient, and the patient is not aware that the pharmacist is stepping away from the situation. Whether another pharmacist on duty completes the prescription or patients are proactively directed to pharmacies where certain therapy is available, or even different systems are set up, the patient gets the medication, and the pharmacist steps away from that activity, with no intersection between the two.

This means that pharmacists who are actively and publicly (or to the patient) stating they will *not* provide EC *are* in violation of that code and how it is to be implemented. . . .

You can see that all of this is very tangled and incredibly confusing. Some of why is because most of these refusals are very much *only* applied to contraception and/or emergency contraception and to women. These pharmacists are not refusing other patients medications, nor are their personal feelings and/or religious or personal morals often being applied in other areas. For that reason, everyone is being very skirty about the issue, likely to avoid lawsuits and loss of their jobs based on clear sexual discrimination. For that reason, many pharmacists refusing are stating the refusal to be on religious grounds, even if it is not in fact the case, and even if they are not refusing other methods of contraception on those same grounds, which is clearly hypocritical, illogical, sexist and often simply willfully ignorant.

Suffice it to say, it will likely take some time for clearer, broader policies, both in states and federally, and via professional boards for pharmacists and pharmacies, to be sorted out. Unfortunately, it is anticipated that the rates of refusal will continue to increase as more women become aware of Plan B and more women request it.

Ann Telnaes Editorial Cartoon used with the permission of Ann Telnaes, Women's eNews and the Cartoonist Group. All rights reserved.

So, what should I do if my prescription is refused, or if I am over 18 and a pharmacy will not sell me EC over the counter?

You have several options.

First, you may and should demand that another pharmacist fills your prescription or provides you with EC over the counter if you are 18 or over. If the pharmacist refuses to ask someone else, you can ask to speak to a manager and inform them of the required transfer policy.

If that pharmacy refuses outright, you may request they have another pharmacy send the EC to your home via an express shipping agency (at their expense), or that they call into another local pharmacy for your prescription where you can pick it up there.

You can send a letter to your state representative, and to the pharmacy itself, as well as the pharmacy board of your state. If it is a corporate chain, send it to both the local branch you were at and to that chain's corporate HQ [headquarters]. If you want to take an extra stand, make a point of asking the pharmacist who refuses you for those addresses and his/her full name at the time of the refusal, and make clear you are sending a letter.

You may consult a private lawyer to determine if you have grounds for a lawsuit, if you like.

Sometimes, these refusals may turn volatile or be deeply distressing. For instance, the NWLC listed examples of refusals in this document, including a mother of six in Wisconsin who was publicly and loudly called a murderer by her pharmacist in requesting EC, and a rape survivor in Texas who was refused by three different pharmacies.

So, when deciding what to do, be sure and take care of yourself *and* think in your best interest. If you feel up to making a big stand, that's great. But if you'd feel better going to get a friend first, do. If you're just upset enough as it is, let it go, write letters later when you feel up to it. And if making a stand right there and then will put you at risk of not getting EC in time, get the EC first elsewhere, deal with the refusal activism later.

ELEVEN

Morning-After Pills Harm Women and Adolescent Girls

Wendy Wright

In 2010 the Food and Drug Administration approved the sale of emergency contraception pill Ella—the brand name for ulipristal acetate, which is several times more effective than Plan B—with a physician's prescription. Wendy Wright, president and chief executive officer of Concerned Women for America (CWA), argues in the following selection that Ella is an abortion drug in the disguise of a morning-after pill. She describes its similarities to RU-486, an abortion pill that resulted in more than a thousand reported complications, including deaths. The widespread availability of Ella not only threatens the health of patients who use and misuse it, but Wright contends, it also puts pregnancies at risk and encourages the victimization of women with the abortion-inducing drug. CWA is a Christian public policy group that promotes abstinence until marriage and opposes abortion.

Should a drug that is similar to RU-486, the abortion drug, be approved as a morning-after pill? The Food and Drug Administration (FDA) will decide whether to approve ulipristal acetate (under the brand name Ella) as a prescription drug to be used up to five days after intercourse.

Ulipristal, or Ella, is similar to mifepristone (RU-486), a drug that causes an abortion. If the FDA approves Ella, it will combine the serious medical and ethical issues of RU-486 with the troubling problems of the morning-after pill.

At an FDA Advisory Committee hearing, the drug sponsor avoided answering whether the drug causes an abortion—even when repeatedly asked.

Dr. Jeffrey Bray, a pharmacologist at the Food and Drug Administration, said that Ella may both delay ovulation and prohibit embryos from implantation in the uterus. Dr. Scott Emerson, a member of the FDA Advisory Committee and professor of biostatistics at the University of Washington, pressed the drug sponsor on why Ella is more effective the later it is taken. He asserted that any drug must do more than delay ovulation if it can prevent pregnancy up to five days after sex.

Despite this, the panel voted unanimously not to inform people that the drug can do something other than prevent pregnancy by delaying ovulation and that it may cause an abortion. Dr. Melissa Gilliam stated there should be "no extra burdens due to the mechanism of action."

While the drug sponsor, HRA Pharma, is not currently requesting non-prescription access, approval of the drug is the first step to gaining such status. Advocates of "reproductive health" have forthrightly stated that their goal is to make abortion easily and directly accessible without medical oversight or safety protocols.

Dr. Valerie Montgomery Rice, an FDA panel member and dean of Meharry Medical College, insisted the drug should be over-the-counter, asking, "Why would we not move to O.T.C. [over-the-counter] status?"

Ella Is Chemically Similar to RU-486

Ella operates in the same manner as the abortion drug RU-486 by blocking progesterone receptors. RU-486 was approved without adequate trials and, even with restricted distribution, has resulted in thousands of complications including deaths. Over one thousand adverse events from RU-486 have been reported to the FDA. The most frequent were hemorrhage and infection. Most disturbing are seven deaths. In addition, as of 2006, the FDA reported nine life-threatening incidents, 232 hospitalizations, 116 blood transfusions, and 88 cases of infection. This is the minimum number since many people, including doctors, are not willing or unaware of how to report adverse events.

A series of deaths linked to RU-486 of previously healthy women from a rare form of bacterial infection forced the FDA to convene a medical symposium to investigate. The FDA did not foresee this fatal complication, perhaps because the appropriate trials and information were not required or submitted to the FDA prior to its approval of RU-486.

Even though the FDA placed restrictions on administering RU-486, abortion providers flagrantly violated the protocol. Planned Parenthood openly posts its deviations from the FDA's protocol on its websites. (Holly Patterson, a healthy 18-year-old, died from a Planned Parenthood administered RU-486 abortion. She had visited the organization's website, where it claimed that RU-486 was "extremely safe.") FDA officials could not or would not enforce their restrictions.

The lesson is quite clear: abortion providers, or those who seek to cause an abortion on a woman, are willing to ignore FDA guidelines and endanger women's lives and health. Instituting regulations on a drug that can end a pregnancy will not restrain those who are intent on aborting a woman's baby. While advocates for RU-486 may claim it is safe, the families of the women who died from the drug will beg to differ.

Ella's Possible Risks to Women

The clinical trials looked at by the European Medicines Agency (EMA) reported on a single dose per menstrual cycle in a limited group of women. In the real world, it will be used more frequently and by all types of females. Of particular concern are adolescents and those less capable of understanding the complicated language on a drug label (i.e. non-English speakers).

The abortion pill RU-486 is marketed as Mifeprex. Many think ulipristal (brand name Ella) is similar to RU-486, the use of which resulted in more than one thousand reported complications, including death.

Women or girls who are fearful of a pregnancy will be inclined to take a double dose or repeated doses within a month, going to different doctors or pharmacies if necessary.

EMA noticed an effect on all tissues, particularly the liver, "if the drug is used again a month later. Most likely this has no implications, because ulipristal acetate is given as a single dose, but in repeated dose this could result in toxicity due to accumulation."

The clinical trials report a pattern of infections and bleeding disturbances that are similar to the complications reported for RU-486. Pain and bleeding are also the warning signals of an ectopic pregnancy. One known RU-486 fatality was a patient who died from a ruptured ectopic pregnancy. Brenda Vise called the abortion provider numerous times to report pain and bleeding. She was told these are the usual effects of RU-486 and not to go to a hospital. By the time she went to a hospital, it was too late. Women taking Ella may mistake the signs of an ectopic pregnancy and not receive critical medical care.

The subjects in the clinical trials were females 16 years and older. However, if Ella is approved, it will be taken by girls younger than 16. Adolescents are especially vulnerable to relying on it as a regular form of birth control, because they generally don't plan ahead or don't want to admit they're regularly having sex.

Also missing in the trials are women with anemia or respiratory disease and women who are already using hormonal contraceptives who may take Ella for missed pills. The selected subjects do not reflect the widespread types of women who will use the drug who think that an FDA approval assures it is safe for all women.

Ella's Possible Risk on Pregnancies

The lack of adequate trials leaves open the question as to whether Ella is teratogenic [birth-defect-causing] and what kinds of birth defects it may cause in surviving or subsequent pregnancies. In the Phase III trials, 49 of the women who took Ella became pregnant, 31 had induced abortions, 11 had spontaneous abortions, two had live births (one baby suffered optic nerve hypoplasia and developmental delay), and five were lost to follow-up. There was no indication if the babies who were aborted or miscarried suffered defects.

The EMA admitted, "Extremely limited data are available on the health of the foetus/new-born in case a pregnancy is exposed to ulipristal acetate." It also noted, "The safety for a human embryo is unknown."

Although voting unanimously on the drug's safety, several panel members expressed concern that there is not enough information on the drug's effect on a pregnancy.

But then the FDA panel "strongly recommended" that the FDA not require a pregnancy test before taking the drug, instead making women rely on a doctor's opinion on whether they're pregnant.

Why would the panel insist on not ensuring that a woman is not pregnant before taking Ella? It's possible a woman could be pregnant from a previous sexual encounter. Why do they want women and researchers to be in the dark, not fully certain whether she is pregnant when she takes Ella? Perhaps to avert liability from the drug company if a woman later miscarries, her surviving baby suffers health issues or to deceive women on whether Ella caused them to abort a baby.

If Ella is approved, there is no adequate reporting mechanism to ascertain the numbers and kinds of complications women or their surviving and subsequent babies are likely to experience. This can leave the false impression that the drug is safe and effective when, in reality, complications are not reported or made available for women to make an informed decision.

One FDA committee member, Dr. Melissa Gilliam, argued against long-term studies on pregnancy outcomes. She claimed it would be "biased" because people who experience a negative effect are more likely to report. This reveals a deep distrust of women and allowing women to have full information. While researchers may want statistical minutiae, mothers care more about what kind of effect a drug may have on their baby.

The FDA panel exposes the radical view of many in the "reproductive health" community who view pregnancy as the worst

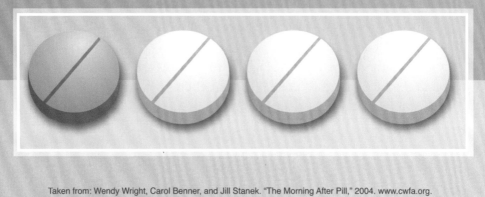

Up to One in Four Pregnancies May Occur if the Morning-After Pill Is Used

Taken from: Wendy Wright, Carol Benner, and Jill Stanek. "The Morning After Pill," 2004. www.cwfa.org.

possible condition, and any negative effect caused by a drug on women and babies is merely collateral damage.

Interestingly, the panel chairman Dr. Sandra Carson strongly recommended that the drug label restrict use by lactating mothers. This clearly indicates that she believes the drug could have an effect on a nursing baby. It's only common sense, then, that babies *in utero*, receiving nutrition and oxygen from their mothers, may also be affected by the drug.

Abortifacient Effect and Lack of Informed Consent

Ella blocks progesterone receptors, causing a hostile environment for an embryo by interfering with the uterine lining so that an embryo cannot implant or, if implanted, not receive nutrition.

The EMA states, "Ella is contra-indicated during an existing or suspected pregnancy." However, most women would not know if they are pregnant at an early phase of the pregnancy.

If Ella is easy to obtain, it will be used past 120 hours. A large selling point of Ella is the claim that it is effective for a longer time postcoitally than Plan B. Women and predators will be enticed to use it beyond 120 hours, putting the woman at greater risk of aborting an implanted embryo (by any definition, a pregnancy).

Women who are led to believe that Ella is a "morning-after pill" may find out too late it may have aborted their baby, causing them emotional and psychological harm. Not providing women full information will be viewed as a deliberate effort to manipulate women for profit or ideological purposes.

Abuse of Easily Obtained Reproductive Drugs

If Ella is easy to obtain, women will be victims to it being slipped to them without their consent. A pattern of abuse has already emerged with abortion-inducing drugs.

Reports (compiled by Life Issues Institute, *LifeNews*, *Life-SiteNews* and Concerned Women for America) include:

- In 2007, a 21-year-old Virginia man was sentenced to five years in prison for trying to poison his girlfriend with the intent of trying to cause an abortion. Daniel Riase crushed two misoprostol pills and put them into 19-year-old Sharii Best's drink, after which she began to bleed. She went to the hospital, where her 11-week pregnancy ended in miscarriage. She later discovered an e-mail receipt for his purchase of the drug.
- In 2007, a 34-year-old Wisconsin man named Manish Patel was arrested and charged with attempted first-degree homicide of an unborn child for trying to cause the abortion of his unborn twins. He obtained mifepristone (RU-486) from his native India and put it in his girlfriend's drink. Darshana Patel never drank the spiked drink, but turned it over to the authorities after suspecting foul play. Testing confirmed the presence of the drug. She believes a previous miscarriage was also caused by Manish slipping the drug in her drink.
- In 2009 in Alaska, Airman First Class Scott Boie faced a court martial for causing his wife to have an abortion. He did

a computer search and got a friend to obtain misoprostol for him. He crushed up the pills and put them in his wife Caylinn's food. She miscarried a week later, thinking it occurred naturally. She learned about his actions from a friend.

- In 2010, 38-year-old New York pharmacist Orbin Eeli Tercero was arrested for causing his Pennsylvania girlfriend to have an abortion. He allegedly inserted misoprostol tablets vaginally during two sexual encounters. He also dissolved misoprostol tablets in her drinks. As she started miscarrying, she discovered the partially dissolved pill in her discharge. He is charged with the murder of an unborn child in the first degree.

- In 2010, 31-year-old Jered Ahlstrom from Utah pleaded guilty to unlawful termination of his girlfriend's pregnancy. He put misoprostol in her food twice to cause an abortion. She delivered a 16-week stillborn baby. He later admitted over e-mail that he had caused her abortion.

- In 2007, a 25-year-old Maryland man, William Stanley Sutton, spiked his girlfriend's drink in an attempt to cause an abortion. He used a cattle hormone sometimes used to cause abortions in cows. Lauren Ashley Tucker went to the hospital complaining of a possible poisoning after consuming the foul drink that burned her throat. Both she and her 15-week-old unborn baby survived. He was charged with reckless endangerment, assault, and contaminating her drink.

- The girlfriend of a Canadian man, Gary Bourgeois, refused to have an abortion. During sexual relations, he inserted misoprostol. Later she experienced violent cramps, then felt a partly dissolved pill drop from her vagina. Her baby died. In September 2003, he pleaded guilty to aggravated assault and administering a noxious substance.

- Dr. Stephen Pack pled guilty to injecting Joy Schepis with an abortion-inducing drug in April 2000. The New York doctor jabbed his former lover with a syringe filled with methotrexate to cause an abortion because she refused to have one.

These cases are known because charges were filed. No one knows how many other women suffered "miscarriages" or abortions forced upon them by someone else.

The EMA assumed a warning on a label that "use of ulipristal acetate is not recommended in females with severe hepatic impairment, is . . . considered sufficient." The EMA also restricts use by those with severe asthma. Label warnings of contra-indications will not necessarily deter a predator whose goal is to prevent or end a woman's pregnancy.

Easy to access abortion drugs, while touted as giving women more control over their bodies, are just as easily used by men to exploit women.

Abuse of Minors

Minors who are sexually [active] are oftentimes victims of sexual abuse. Interaction with medical professionals is an important line of defense. Making Ella easy to obtain will remove a critical opportunity for abused minors to get the real help that they need.

The Alan Guttmacher Institute reported: "The younger women are when they first have intercourse the more likely they are to have had unwanted or nonvoluntary first sex, seven in 10 of those who had sex before age 13, for example."

"The possibility of sexual abuse should be considered routinely in every adolescent female patient who has initiated sexual activity," stated Dr. Joycelyn Elders in the *Journal of the American Medical Association*. The rush to choose "pregnancy outcome options" may preempt efforts to rule out sexual abuse. "Sexual abuse is a common antecedent of adolescent pregnancy, with up to 66% of pregnant teens reporting histories of abuse. . . . Pregnancy may also be a sign of ongoing sexual abuse. . . . [Researchers] found that of 535 young women who were pregnant, 44% had been raped, of whom 11% became pregnant as a result of the rape. One half of these young women with rape histories were raped more than once."

Pill's Approval Is Based on False Promises

Many lessons can be learned from the approval of the morning-after pill Plan B—and should not be repeated.

Advocates for the morning-after pill claimed that it would dramatically reduce pregnancies and abortions. Planned Parenthood states that the morning-after pill "could prevent 1.7 million unintended pregnancies and 800,000 abortions each year in the U.S." That would mean reducing abortions by fifty percent. Claims like this won support inside and outside the FDA, yet the reality is quite different.

Advocates have since admitted that easy access to the morning-after pill does not reduce pregnancies or abortions.

Dr. James Trussell, an aggressive proponent of "emergency contraceptive pills" (ECP), concluded in several studies subsequent to the FDA's approval that easy access to the morning-after pill has not reduced pregnancies or abortions. His most recent analysis in May 2010 stated, "No published study has yet demonstrated that increasing access to ECPs can reduce pregnancy or abortion rates in a population although one demonstration project and three clinical trials were specifically designed to address this issue." This is true even when women are given advance supplies of the drug.

Concerned Women for America had warned that easy access to the morning-after pill would not reduce pregnancies or abortions, but lead to women relying on it (the least effective form of contraception) as a regular form of birth control and multiple use.

Dr. Trussell reluctantly admits that "reanalysis of one of the randomized trials suggests that easier access to ECPs may have increased the frequency of coital acts with the potential to lead to pregnancy. Women in the increased access group were significantly more likely to report that they had ever used emergency contraception because they did not want to use either condoms or another contraceptive method. Increased access to EC had a greater impact on repeat use among women who were at lower baseline risk of pregnancy."

Moreover, previous studies (certainly some that the FDA relied on) miscalculated estimates of the effectiveness of morning-after pills. As Dr. Trussell put it, "The risk of pregnancy for women requesting ECPs appears to be lower than assumed in the estimates of ECP efficacy, which are consequently likely to be overestimates."

Ideology Trumping Women's Health

Abortion advocates cloak abortion-causing drugs as a woman's "right." This is a facade used to promote their own ideological crusade. With Ella, women will be enticed to buy a poorly tested abortion drug under the guise that it's a morning-after pill. The FDA should not unleash Ella on unsuspecting women, a drug promoted by activists with a history of overstating the efficacy of reproductive drugs while understating the overall risks to women.

TWELVE

Intrauterine Devices Are Underused by Adolescent Girls

John Sanford

An intrauterine device (IUD) is a form of birth control inserted in the uterus. Shaped like the letter T, the device is either copper-based or hormonal and can prevent pregnancy for years at a time. In the following selection medical writer John Sanford states that teenage girls underuse IUDs although they are safe, effective, and more convenient than birth control pills. Myths that they are not appropriate for women who have not yet given birth and increase the risk of pelvic inflammatory disease discourage usage. In addition, Sanford claims that many teens are unaware of IUDs as a contraceptive option.

Only a tiny percentage of teenage girls in the United States use intrauterine devices [IUDs] for birth control, even though studies show they are safe, effective and very low-maintenance, according to researchers at Lucile Packard Children's Hospital and the School of Medicine [at Stanford University].

In a paper published [in June 2010] in the *Journal of Pediatric and Adolescent Gynecology,* lead author Sophia Yen, MD, MPH, a board-certified specialist in adolescent medicine at Packard Children's, and her co-authors report that more than a dozen studies have shown that teenagers with IUDs were as likely or more likely to continue using them compared with teens using birth-control pills. Furthermore, IUDs can work for as long as five or 10 years, depending on the type; are cost-effective; and are more than 99-percent effective at preventing pregnancy, the authors note.

"IUDs are a good contraceptive option for teens," said the paper's senior author, Paula Hillard, MD, a pediatric gynecologist at Packard Children's and a professor of obstetrics and gynecology at the medical school.

An intrauterine device is a form of birth control that, after insertion into the uterus, can prevent pregnancy with 99 percent effectiveness for an extended period of time, studies show.

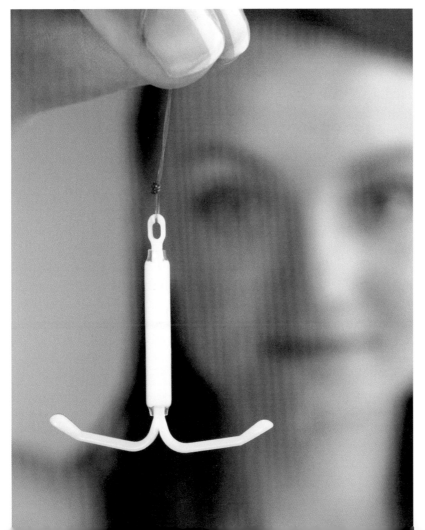

Still, only a very small number of adolescents choose this contraceptive option. From 2006 to 2008, 1 percent of U.S. girls ages 15–19 used IUDs for birth control, while 15.2 percent used birth-control pills, according to the National Survey of Family Growth. (Among U.S. women ages 15–44, 3.4 percent used IUDs and 17.3 percent used the pill from 2006 to 2008.)

Myths About the IUD

"The IUD has an undeserved bad reputation both in the public and among physicians," said Yen, who is also a clinical instructor in pediatrics. "There's the myth that they're not appropriate for women who haven't yet given birth, and the myth that they increase the risk of pelvic inflammatory disease." The first myth, she said, is likely a vestige of early liability fears: Doctors wanted to make sure a woman had already had a baby to avoid possible lawsuits alleging that an IUD had rendered her infertile. Countering this myth, the authors highlight the 2006 British adaptation of the World Health Organization Medical Eligibility

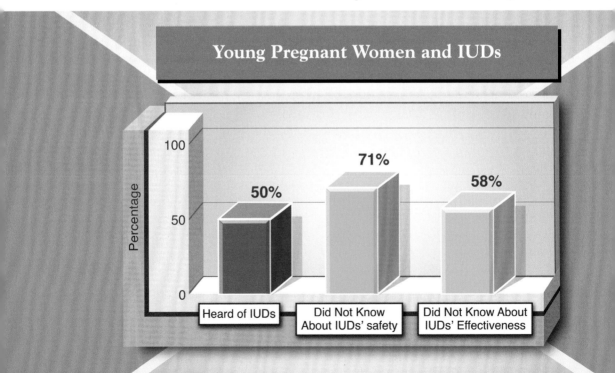

Taken from: N.L. Standwood and K.A. Bradley. "Young Pregnant Women's Knowledge of Modern Intrauterine Devices." *Obstetrics & Gynecology*, December 2006.

Criteria for contraception, which states that previous IUD use is not associated with reduced fertility.

The second myth likely stems from the notoriety of a popular IUD brand marketed in the 1970s. "Some mothers of today's teenagers remember the Dalkon Shield, which was associated with a significant risk of infection and basically gave IUDs a bad name," said Hillard. "So there is some of that lingering concern."

Studies show a slightly increased risk of pelvic inflammatory disease [PID] during the first month after IUD insertion. This risk is likely due to bacteria—either those normally living in the vagina or those from a sexually transmitted disease—that can be carried into the uterus when the IUD is inserted. But beyond that initial interval, women who have IUDs are at no greater risk for PID than women who don't have them.

For some young women, the insertion can cause moderate discomfort and, in some cases, severe pain, the researchers say. Physicians can administer a painkiller or local anesthetic to make the process more tolerable. For a couple of months after insertion, some women may feel uterine tenderness akin to menstrual cramps.

Well Suited for Teenagers

According to the paper, however, many adolescents either don't know about IUDs or else have serious reservations about them. "In one survey, 60 percent of adolescents were unaware of IUDs as a contraceptive option," the authors write. "Anecdotally, size is one of the most frequent questions asked at the first IUD evaluation visit."

IUDs are slender T-shaped objects—about half the length of your index finger. The placement of the device is probably one source of trepidation for adolescents. "It's just the fear of having something in your uterus," Yen said.

Hillard noted that IUDs are as effective as sterilization but are entirely reversible. Both she and Yen emphasized that IUDs should be used with condoms to prevent the acquisition and spread of sexually transmitted diseases.

On the whole, the authors assert that IUDs are especially well-suited for teenagers. "Adolescents may have difficulty with consistent oral contraceptive use, and are at a particularly high risk for unintended pregnancy with resultant negative consequences to their lives," they conclude. "Thus, IUDs are appropriate for adolescents, as many would like to avoid pregnancy for five or more years to allow completion of educational or career goals."

What You Should Know About Birth Control

Facts About Birth Control and Women in the United States

According to the Guttmacher Institute:

- Sixty-two million women in the nation are of childbearing age (fifteen to forty-four).
- In order for a woman to have only two children, she must use birth control for about three decades.
- More than 99 percent of women aged fifteen to forty-four who have had sexual intercourse have used birth control at least once.
- Teen women aged fifteen to nineteen who do not use birth control the first time they have sex are twice as likely to become teen mothers than those who use it.
- Twenty-three percent of women who use birth control depend on condoms as their primary method. The use of condoms is higher among women aged twenty to twenty-four and lower among married and older women.
- Fifty-four percent of the 2.9 million teen women who use birth control, or 1.5 million, depend on the pill.

Facts About Condoms

According to Advocates for Youth:

- In one year, only two out of a hundred couples who use condoms correctly and consistently will have an unplanned pregnancy.

- In one year of using male condoms correctly and consistently, 98 percent of women will not get pregnant. For typical use, 85 percent of women will not get pregnant.
- In one year of using female condoms correctly and consistently, 95 percent of women will not get pregnant. For typical use, 79 percent of women will not get pregnant.
- By comparison, in one year, 15 percent of women who use no form of birth control will not get pregnant.

Facts About the Birth Control Pill

According to Planned Parenthood:
- In one year, fewer than one out of a hundred women will have an unplanned pregnancy if they take the pill daily as directed.
- In one year, around nine out of a hundred women will have an unplanned pregnancy if they do not take the pill daily as directed.
- The pill may be slightly less effective for overweight women.
- The following drugs and supplements may make the pill less effective: The antibiotic rifampin, some oral medications for yeast infections, some HIV (AIDS virus) medications, some antiseizure medications, and Saint-John's-wort.
- Diarrhea and vomiting can reduce the pill's effectiveness, and other forms of birth control (i.e., condom, diaphragm, sponge) should also be used until the problem is addressed.
- It may take from one to six months (in some cases) for a woman's period to become regular after she stops taking the pill.
- Rare but serious and potentially lethal problems—particularly for combination pill takers—include stroke; heart attack; blood clot in the legs, lungs, heart, or brain; high blood pressure; jaundice; liver tumors; and gallstones.

Facts About Intrauterine Devices (IUDs)

According to the Office of Population Affairs, US Department of Health and Human Services:

- An IUD is placed in the uterus by a physician at a clinic.
- The ParaGard Intrauterine Copper Contraceptive, or Copper T IUD, is made with copper and plastic and blocks sperm from reaching and fertilizing an egg to prevent pregnancy.
- Mirena Intrauterine System (IUS) also blocks sperm from reaching and fertilizing an egg and releases the hormone progestin (found in birth control pills), which stops the ovaries from releasing an egg.
- ParaGard IUDs are effective for at least ten years; the Mirena IUS at least five years.
- The ParaGard IUD can be used as emergency contraception if inserted within five days after unprotected sexual intercourse.
- One out of a hundred women using an IUD will have an unplanned pregnancy.

What You Should Do About Birth Control

Be Curious

From the male condom to the intrauterine device (IUD), birth control is surrounded by a lot of myths and misconceptions. When it comes to the numbers and statistics on contraceptives and their effectiveness, adults often disagree on their accuracy or validity. Conflicting studies also make their way into the discussions and debates on birth control, which can add to the confusion. And the Internet, as you already know, can be just as valuable as misleading as a source of information.

Whether it is comprehensive or abstinence-only, sex education in health class can cover a good deal of information. But you are bound to have questions, concerns, and even doubts about birth control and contraceptives when the lessons are over. How can you tell what information is correct or what is not? You should be curious. Most teens are independent thinkers, and, through curiosity, you can take further steps to inform yourself. For instance, if you come across a new study about birth control in the news, read beyond the headlines and find out how the research led to the findings. Or if you find statistics on contraceptives that seem too good—or bad—to be true, be your own fact checker and try to verify them using multiple sources. The following websites about sex and birth control were created with teens in mind: Stay Teen, a site from the National Campaign to Prevent Teen and Unplanned Pregnancy; Scarleteen, a site and blog that supports comprehensive sex education; and TeensHealth, a site by the Nemours Center for Children's Health Media that offers birth control information and advice. A library or bookstore near you will offer a selection of books on contraception and sex for teens as well.

Older people whom you know and trust—friends, siblings, and relatives—can provide some information, especially if you are seeking practical knowledge or firsthand experience about birth control. But if you need medical advice or have health-related questions involving the use of contraceptives, your best bet is to have a discussion with your physician or school nurse, who can refer you to a qualified expert or specialist if necessary.

Be Empowered

Teens and birth control continues to be debated by policy makers, advocates, and parents. Some adults may object to it on ethical or religious grounds. However, it is important to know that state and federal laws protect teens' access to contraception. In the United States, minors are able to use family planning services without parental consent under federal Title X funding. Legislation in some states has tried to challenge this right, but none at this time has repealed it.

As long as the protections of Title X funding remain, teens have the right to confidential access to birth control at clinics or family planning centers. Also, some might not realize that there are no age restrictions on the sale of condoms. As for getting emergency contraception, in 2009 the US Food and Drug Administration allowed the over-the-counter sale of Plan B to seventeen-year-olds without a prescription and those under seventeen with a prescription. If a pharmacist refuses to sell emergency contraception to you and you are either seventeen or have a prescription, you can take several steps, such as requesting the service of another pharmacist or to speak to a manager. An article in this volume discusses more actions you can take, but if you need emergency contraception, obtaining it in a timely manner is a priority.

If you are in opposition to Plan B, you can also take action. You can contact Concerned Women of America, which is active in all fifty states, or similar organizations to find out what you can do (e.g., sign a petition or join a campaign) to advocate against the availability of emergency contraception. Additionally, you can promote abstinence in your community and among your peers by joining an organization such as True Love Waits or a church youth group.

Whatever your position on birth control, which can change over time, it can be strengthened by learning the other side's arguments. Listen and read with an open mind, and use your opponents' positions, evidence, and beliefs to structure your own arguments.

Be Safe

The grown-up consequences of having sex—particularly the chance of an unplanned pregnancy—are reasons enough for many teens to abstain from sex and, if in a relationship, be intimate with their partners in nonsexual ways or without intercourse. For those teens who choose to have sex and use birth control, it is of utmost importance to use the method consistently and correctly. It only takes one mistake to reduce or eliminate altogether the effectiveness of a contraceptive.

Therefore, you must use your contraceptive always and only as directed. If it is a condom, that means using it correctly and using one every time you have sex, following the instructions for use. If it is a pill, that means taking it every day as instructed by your physician. It must be noted that only condoms and latex barriers can prevent sexually transmitted diseases. Using them as a backup method can provide extra assurance. But no matter how careful you are, no form of birth control is 100 percent guaranteed to prevent pregnancy.

If you decide to take the pill or other types of hormonal birth control (injections, vaginal ring, the Mirena IUD), it is also important to keep in mind the harmful interactions with other drugs and the potential side effects. Since side effects can be lethal in rare cases, bring anything out of the ordinary that you experience to the attention of your physician.

ORGANIZATIONS TO CONTACT

The editors have compiled the following list of organizations concerned with the issues debated in this book. The descriptions are derived from materials provided by the organizations. All have publications or information available for interested readers. The list was compiled on the date of publication of the present volume; names, addresses, phone and fax numbers, and e-mail and Internet addresses may change. Be aware that many organizations take several weeks or longer to respond to inquiries, so allow as much time as possible.

Advocates for Youth
2000 M St. NW, Ste. 750, Washington, DC 20036
(202) 419-3420 • fax: (202) 419-1448
website: www.advocatesforyouth.org

Formerly the Center for Population Options, Advocates for Youth is the only national organization focusing solely on pregnancy and HIV prevention among young people. It provides information, education, and advocacy to youth-serving agencies and professionals, policy makers, and the media. Among the organization's numerous publications are "Comprehensive Sex Education: Research and Results" and "Reproductive Health Outcomes & Contraceptive Use Among US Teens." Education programs, brochures, posters, videos, reports, manuals and policy briefs are also available on or through its website.

The Alan Guttmacher Institute (AGI)
125 Maiden Ln., 7th Fl., New York, NY 10038
(212) 248-1111 • fax: (212) 248-1951
website: www.guttmacher.org

The institute works to protect and expand the reproductive choices of all women and men. It strives to ensure people's access to the information and services they need to exercise their rights and responsibilities concerning sexual activity, reproduction, and family planning. Among the institute's publications are the periodicals *Perspectives on Sexual and Reproductive Health, International Family Planning Perspectives,* and *Guttmacher Policy Review.* The institute also provides media kits, fact sheets, slide presentations, reports, and statistics on its website as well as a "tablemaker" feature that allows one to build customized statistical tables.

Child Trends
4301 Connecticut Ave. NW, Ste. 350, Washington, DC 20008
(202) 572-6000 • fax: (202) 362-8420
website: www.childtrends.org

Child Trends works to provide accurate statistical and research information regarding children and their families in the United States and to educate the American public on the ways existing social trends—such as the increasing rate of teenage pregnancy—affect children. In addition to the newsletter *Facts at a Glance,* which presents the latest data on teen pregnancy rates for every state, the organization also publishes fact sheets such as "Condom Use and Consistency Among Teen Males" and "Trends and Recent Estimates: Contraceptive Use Among US Teens and Young Adults," as well as reports, research, speeches, presentations, and briefings.

Children's Aid Society (CAS)
105 E. Twenty-Second St., New York, NY 10010
(212) 949-4800
website: www.childrensaidsociety.org

In 1984 Dr. Michael A. Carrera and the CAS developed an Adolescent Pregnancy Prevention Program that uses a holistic approach to empower youth. The program's objective is to help teens develop personal goals and the desire for a productive future, in addition to developing their sexual literacy and educating them about the consequences of sexual activity. This program works with boys and girls from the age of eleven or twelve and follows them through high school and beyond. Guided by a philosophy that sees youth as "at promise" instead of "at risk," the program works to develop a participant's capacity and desire to avoid pregnancy. The program model provides opportunities for young people to discover their interests and develop their talents, plus it emphasizes education and employment.

Concerned Women for America (CWA)
1015 Fifteenth St. NW, Ste. 1100, Washington, DC 20005
(202) 488-7000 • fax: (202) 488-0806
website: www.cwfa.org

CWA's purpose is to preserve, protect, and promote traditional Judeo-Christian values through education, legislative action, and other activities. It is concerned with creating an environment that is conducive to building strong families and raising healthy children. The organization opposes the morning-after pill and supports abstinence as the best birth control for youths. CWA publishes the monthly *Family Voice*, which periodically addresses issues such as abortion and promoting sexual abstinence in schools.

Family Research Council
801 G St. NW, Washington, DC 20001
(202) 393-2100 • fax: (202) 393-2134
website: www.frc.org

The council seeks to promote and protect the interests of the traditional family. It focuses on issues such as parental autonomy and responsibility, community support for single parents, and adolescent pregnancy. Among the council's numerous publications are the papers "Why Wait: The Benefits of Abstinence Before Marriage" and "Spending Too Little on Abstinence."

Focus on the Family
8605 Explorer Dr., Colorado Springs, CO 80920
(719) 531-5181 • fax: (719) 531-3424
website: www.focusonthefamily.com

Focus on the Family is a Christian organization dedicated to preserving and strengthening the traditional family. It believes that the breakdown of the traditional family is in part linked to teen pregnancy. The organization publishes *Citizen* magazine, which discusses current social issues; an e-newsletter; and online articles such as "Abstinence Education" and "Abstinence Before Marriage."

The Heritage Foundation
214 Massachusetts Ave. NE, Washington, DC 20002
(202) 546-4400
e-mail: info@heritage.org • website: www.heritage.org

The Heritage Foundation is a public policy research institute that supports the ideas of limited government and the free-market system. It promotes the view that the welfare system has contributed to the problems of illegitimacy and teenage pregnancy. Among the foundation's numerous publications is its Backgrounder series, which includes papers such as "Evidence on the Effectiveness of Abstinence Education: An Update" and "Reforming Health Care to Protect Parents' Rights." It also publishes commentary and blog posts about teen pregnancy and minors' access to birth control.

It's Your (Sex) Life
e-mail: think@mtv.com • website: www.itsyoursexlife.com

It's Your (Sex) Life is the website of an information campaign sponsored by a partnership between MTV and the Kaiser Family Foundation. It offers access to videos, articles, news, interactive quizzes, and groups that provide information on sex, contraception, and safe sex. The Get Yourself Tested (GYT) toolkit and *Your Guide to Safe & Responsible Sex* is also available.

National Campaign to Prevent Teen and Unplanned Pregnancy
1776 Massachusetts Ave. NW, Ste. 200, Washington, DC 20036
(202) 478-8500 • fax: (212) 478-8588
websites: www.thenationalcampaign.org • www.stayteen.org

The National Campaign to Prevent Teen and Unplanned Pregnancy seeks to improve the lives and future prospects of children and families and, in particular, to help ensure that children are born into stable, two-parent families who are committed to and ready for the demanding task of raising the next generation. Its specific strategy is to prevent teen pregnancy and unplanned pregnancy among single young adults. It supports a combination of responsible values and behaviors by both men and women and responsible policies in both the public and private sectors. The organization publishes national and state statistics, provides articles such as "With One Voice 2010: America's Adults and Teens Sound Off About Teen Pregnancy," and sponsors the National Day to Prevent Teen Pregnancy.

Planned Parenthood Federation of America (PPFA)

434 W. Thirty-Third St., New York, NY 10001
(212) 541-7800 • fax: (212) 245-1845
website: www.plannedparenthood.org

For more than ninety years, Planned Parenthood has promoted a commonsense approach to women's health and well-being, based on respect for each individual's right to make informed, independent decisions about sex, health, and family planning. Among PPFA's numerous publications are the research papers "Emergency Contraception—History and Access" and "The Truth About Condoms," as well as resources for educators.

Sex Information and Education Council of Canada (SIECCAN)

850 Coxwell Ave., Toronto, ON M4C 5R1
(416) 466-5304 • fax: (416) 778-0785
email: sieccan@web.net • website: www.sieccan.org

SIECCAN is a Candian nonprofit organization established in 1964 to foster public and professional education about human sexuality. SIECCAN is dedicated to informing and educating the public and professionals about all aspects of human sexuality in order to support the positive integration of sexuality into people's lives. Its publications include the *Canadian Journal of Human Sexuality*, a quarterly, peer-reviewed journal; *Common Questions About Sexual Health Education*, a resource document published online; *Being Sexual: An Illustrated Series on Sexuality and Relationships*, a seventeen-booklet series to meet the educational needs of people with developmental disabilities or problems with language, learning, and communication.

TeensHealth
website: http://teenshealth.org

The TeensHealth website is for teens who seek information and advice about health, emotions, and life. It is part of the Kids-Health family of websites. These sites, run by the nonprofit Nemours Center for Children's Health Media, provide up-to-date health information that is free of "doctor speak." The TeensHealth website provides medical and safety information on many topics, including sex, contraception, and pregnancy with articles, questions and answers, and quizzes.

BIBLIOGRAPHY

Books

Paul Allen. *Condom: One Small Item, One Giant Impact*. Oxford, UK: New Internationalist, 2007.

Ruth Bell. *Changing Bodies, Changing Lives: A Book for Teens on Sex and Relationships*. Expanded 3rd ed. New York: Three Rivers, 2011.

Aine Collier. *The Humble Little Condom: A History*. Amherst, NY: Prometheus, 2007.

Laura Eldridge. *In Our Control: The Complete Guide to Contraceptive Choices for Women*. New York: Seven Stories, 2010.

Miriam Grossman. *You're Teaching My Child What? A Physician Exposes the Lies of Sex Ed and How They Harm Your Child*. Washington, DC: Regnery, 2009.

Elaine Tyler May. *America and the Pill: A History of Promise, Peril, and Liberation*. New York: Basic, 2010.

Heather Munroe Prescott. *The Morning After: A History of Emergency Contraception in the United States*. Piscataway, NJ: Rutgers University Press, 2011.

Pam Stenzel and Melissa Nesdahl. *Nobody Told Me: What You Need to Know About the Physical and Emotional Consequences of Sex Outside of Marriage*. Ventura, CA: Regal, 2011.

Laura Sessions Stepp. *Unhooked: How Young Women Pursue Sex, Delay Love, and Lose at Both*. New York: Penguin, 2007.

Periodicals and Internet Sources

David Everman. "Education Key to Lower Teen Birth Rates." *Easton (MD) Star Democrat*, October 3, 2011.

William McCleery. "Learning to Wait." *World Magazine*, January 30, 2010.

Meredith Melnick. "Should the Birth-Control Pill Be Sold Without a Prescription?" *Newsweek*, July 7, 2010.

Barbara Miner. "Taking Sex Ed to School." *Utne Reader*, September/ October 2008.

Tara Parker-Pope. "The Myth of Rampant Teenage Promiscuity." *New York Times*, January 26, 2009.

Kate Storm. "Get with the Flow: All About FAM." Scarleteen, February 6, 2008. www.scarleteen.com.

J. Thomas. "Virginity Pledgers Are Just as Likely as Matched Nonpledgers to Report Premarital Intercourse." *Perspectives on Sexual and Reproductive Health*, March 2009.

Charlotte Tucker. "School-Based Health Centers Improving Access for Youth." *Nation's Health*, April 2011.

Joel Turtle. "How Children Are Sexually Corrupted in Public Schools." NewsWithViews.com, September 7, 2008. www .newswithviews.com.

Michelle A. Vu. "Free Condoms for 11-Year-Olds? Philadelphia and Its Sex Problem." *Christian Post*, April 15, 2011.

INDEX

PICTURE CREDITS